Nanny Fran Can, Did & Done!

Francene Alexander

BALBOA.
PRESS

A DIVISION OF HAY HOUSE

Balboa Press books may be ordered through booksellers or by contacting:

Balboa Press
A Division of Hay House
1663 Liberty Drive
Bloomington, IN 47403
www.balboapress.com
1 (877) 407-4847

Because of the dynamic nature of the Internet, any web addresses or links contained in this book may have changed since publication and may no longer be valid. The views expressed in this work are solely those of the author and do not necessarily reflect the views of the publisher, and the publisher hereby disclaims any responsibility for them.

The author of this book does not dispense medical advice or prescribe the use of any technique as a form of treatment for physical, emotional, or medical problems without the advice of a physician, either directly or indirectly. The intent of the author is only to offer information of a general nature to help you in your quest for emotional and spiritual well-being. In the event you use any of the information in this book for yourself, which is your constitutional right, the author and the publisher assume no responsibility for your actions.

Any people depicted in stock imagery provided by Getty Images are models, and such images are being used for illustrative purposes only. Certain stock imagery © Getty Images.

Print information available on the last page.

ISBN: 978-1-9822-3161-3 (sc)
ISBN: 978-1-9822-3160-6 (hc)
ISBN: 978-1-9822-3163-7 (e)

Library of Congress Control Number: 2019909969

Balboa Press rev. date: 08/06/2019

Nanny Fran dedicates this book to everyone who loves, honors and adores all the babies. She wants to especially thank those who rescue, those who feed homeless animals and those pet sitters all over this world who make your babies and the homeless babies their top priority while you are away.

Contents

Foreword

Sometimes, others know the greatness of your life's work, or just maybe they were put in your path for you to be grateful for the work you do that you love.

Nanny Fran can, did, and done!

Nanny Fran's Inspiration

I feel honored to care for all of God's babies.

Animals have such integrity, intelligence, compassion, and love that I feel honored to care for them. They demonstrate daily everywhere in the world that they are kinder to each other, though they may be different species, than we humans are to one another.

I am overjoyed when I am able to sense emotional or physical problems in an animal and bring them to its guardian's attention. Many times, guardians have very busy work schedules and social lives and don't notice some of the smallest signs of illness, depression, and so on in the animals that live with them.

Some of my families swear that I talk to the animals. I don't. But I dearly wish I could.

I am grateful to all who love and adore their babies. In the two years I worked with families who had adopted abused babies from the Alabama Rescue in 1996.

In Opp, Alabama in 1996 the owner of a compound with 600 dogs died. The state of Alabama called in the HSUS to help. They recommended killing all of them. When the HSUS euthanasia teams arrived they saw only frightened, unkempt dogs who were frightened of strangers. They proceeded to get a court order to stop the mass kill. It went through successfully. Then the Humane Societies of Florida, Illinois and Texas started the transportation of those dear ones to their respective states. Three hundred and forty-three arrived in Florida. I adopted two of them.

None of them were mean. All were simply frightened of our urban environment. After being caged with only the caretakers (and abusers) in the dense woods as their home everything about our world was foreign to them.

After having my Amy, HRH Amelia Elizabeth, for a few weeks I visited our Humane Society. I spoke with the director. I told him that I had grown up on the farm and had been around dogs all my life. I said that I had not seen as much fear in any dog as I had seen in my Amelia Elizabeth. I then started a support group for all families who adopted these frightened babies. For two years we held regular meetings and discussed how to make these dear ones feel loved and wanted. This group was tremendous in sharing knowledge.

I met some of the most wonderful families. They turned their lives upside down and inside out to create safe, loving, and permanent homes for many emotionally and physically abused little ones.

I have been furthering my abilities to love and heal all babies whenever possible. Some awesome modalities exist to heal the mind and body that have nothing to do with obedience training or veterinary medicine. This is a kinder, gentler way to heal.

Chapter 1

Nanny Fran Never Sits Still, and Then ...

Here I am still on the knee walker. For the umpteenth time in three months, I nearly fell off it. Yeah, I sure did. Many times, I have been in a hurry or impatient, and when turning the front wheels, I turn them all the way to the right or left and then only the single back wheel is supporting me in a quick turn.

Imagine a border collie riding this thing because that's what's happening. I want to do things now, but it just doesn't happen.

This contraption has taught me patience just as animal photography has taught me patience—to an extent. If I had completely learned that lesson in each area of my existence, I would not still be saving my butt from crashing to the terrazzo floor after three months of flying around on this vehicle. No, it's not gas powered, but I can make it fly when I am hell-bent for election over some issue in this house.

All last week, I stayed in the house, and so far this week, it's been the same. I don't relish showering and dressing and then loading the knee walker into my car. And driving somewhere and unloading it in this ninety-degree heat is exhausting. I have to propel myself with my good foot across an inferno called an asphalt parking lot. Then, after shopping, I have to lift the forty-pound monster back into my car, drive home, and then unload it onto my garage floor so I can propel myself and my packages into my home. That usually means multiple trips with an already weary body.

So many times, I think of going somewhere, and then just a few seconds later, *No* is shouted from somewhere inside my soul.

Clients have stopped calling because the word has gotten out I suppose. I'm just as happy. I'm relishing the opportunity to be home with my children.

Several times today, Whoopie started barking and bringing her rubber bone to me. She was tired of me sitting for hours on the computer and wanted to play. That suited me fine each time as I had a numb posterior.

With three ceiling fans wafting our lovely ninety-degree air through the room, I've been drinking gallons of water, so potty breaks are frequent. Whoopie's barking is another opportunity for me to get up and go to the bathroom.

It's gotten to the point that every time I go to the bathroom, all the dogs follow. They think I'm going in there to let them outside as there is an outside door in that bathroom.

They train us very well, don't they? I have used that phrase a million times whenever animal lovers describe how they interact with their puppies or kitties. They do train us, and we fall for it willingly. We're here to do their bidding, and we all know that from the day they come into our lives. Who can say no to anything with them?

Chapter 2

A Merry Heart, or the Ministry of Cheerfulness

I titled this chapter in part from *The Ministry of Cheerfulness*, a book I got from Jesse Duplantis, and in part from a book I purchased years ago with the title *A Merry Heart Is the Best Medicine*.

My leg—ouch!—is healing and aching while I'm sitting with it elevated as I type. Dr. Bonsal, rest assured that I'm following your instructions to the letter.

I so much wanted to relate this broken-ankle, incapacitated pet-sitter experience because this is the first time in twenty years I've been unable to walk a dog. Even getting in and out of my home has been an exercise in ramp building for my wheelchair. Who would have thought this would ever have happened?

Over all my years of walking dogs, I have tumbled six ways from Sunday over and around animals and tripped over my own two feet by walking along a sidewalk—just like all of us do. However, this is the first time that I've been incapacitated. I won't even go into the lack of income, as you may well guess, or the fact that I've had to give away my sitting assignments to other pet sitters or turn down families who request my services.

I realize how lucky I have been for sixty-five years. Do you have any idea how hard it is to ask for assistance when you have always been a can-do, Johnny-on-the-spot person?

Whoa! For years, I have bragged, "Nanny Fran Can! You betcha, I can do anything. Yes I can." I have had to on numerous occasions.

Each time I'm requested to care for the fur children, I am in charge of a lovely home that entails enormous attention to home security as well as the fur children. Whenever the unexpected happens with the home or fur children, I am the only person on the scene to save the day. "No brag, just fact." I quote John Wayne and Nanny Fran. I have always been proud of my ability to save the day. I have often said that with my instant-decision and instant-action personality, I could be an EMT. I have had zillions of experiences that can corroborate that statement.

Why am I telling you all this Nanny Fran stuff? Because I can get through this too, and very well, thank you.

I am nothing but cheerful because it's not all about me. The first thing I thought of when my leg was broken was, *Who will come and take care of this dear fifteen-year-old Yorkie whom I need to see seven more times and give medications to twice daily before the mother and father come home?*

Priority number one was this sweet fellow. The accident happened at eight thirty in the morning, and he needed another visit at three that afternoon.

Immediately, my thoughts went to a pet-sitter friend who offered to help me in such a situation. I am not going to say that I called her on my way to the ER or in the ER; however, I did call her right after my release. I asked her to continue the care of this sweet fellow and two others. These clients have me come to their homes and walk their dogs each day, so I was immediately at ease.

After the fall, I did have to request assistance from a friend who had just completed her CNA course. God is amazing, isn't he?

Actually, God provided for me in another fashion as well.

One of my longtime clients is a doctor, and when my accident happened, I had no doctor. Well, actually, I used to have a primary care physician, but I found out I was no longer his patient because I'd had no need for his services for the past ten years or so. Then I was told that he could no longer take new patients.

My client referred me to a sports surgeon at her hospital. Thank heaven for her referral. He was amazing. My break involved multiple bones in my ankle. Pins and plates were needed at multiple sites.

I was going back and forth from my home to the hospital nearly every day for a week, and the following week I went in for surgery. Ninety percent of my concerns in those two weeks were for me. Ten percent of my concerns were for the dry and wet cat and dog food as well as kitty litter that had been stored in my home. I asked my wonderful CNA friend to take me to the pet food store to purchase dry dog food. On another occasion, I asked her to stop at Walmart to purchase more dry cat food and some kitty litter.

I had previously stockpiled cans of wet cat food in my front entry closet when they had been on sale, so I had no concerns regarding an adequate supply of wet food.

Without fail, each time, I was assured that all the animals in my business and in my home had adequate provisions and were properly being looked after. I could relax and breathe easier.

The recuperation phase for Nanny Fran is still not all about me. Well, of course not. Whoopie, my golden retriever/basset hound mix, started chewing on the base of her tail to the point that an open sore appeared. It was about two inches in diameter and bright red. Well, I had a broken leg and was unable to physically take her to a vet to be examined. I telephoned a vet tech friend and asked her to please stop over. This precious dear did just that. She gave Whoopie a bath in my dog bathtub and clipped away the hair around the sore. Afterward, we applied colloidal silver gel to the area, put an Elizabethan collar on Whoopie, and started giving her an antibiotic twice daily for seven days. It doesn't sound like there was much to do, but listen to this.

Because of the head collar, Whoopie couldn't drink from the communal water dish on the floor all my other children were using. So multiple times daily, I had to fill a special water bowl that was shaped so that she could drink from it even with the head collar on.

And Whoopie was on prednisone, which makes all animals thirsty as the dickens. So there I was on my knee walker going to the kitchen to get water to pour in Whoopie's special water dish. I was also feeding Whoopie twice daily by hand—dipping her food bowl into the dry kibble, bracing myself on the knee walker, and bending over double with one hand holding her food dish just right so she could have breakfast and dinner while wearing that infernal head collar. I also assumed the same position on the knee walker twice daily as well to give Whoopie a spoonful of peanut butter containing the antibiotic twice daily and the prednisone once daily. I thank God every day that I'm as flexible as Gumby.

Well, halfway through the seven days of this antibiotic administration, I noticed that my kitty, Tabitha, was sneezing. Tabitha is a leukemia-positive kitty who is a delightful and beautiful tuxedo. I learned that I needed to start dosing her with Orbax once daily to help her get over the upper-respiratory infections that occur rather frequently.

The year had been especially hard on her with our extremely high pollen counts. I asked my vet about some kind of medicine for pollen allergies for her. He replied that any medication he could prescribe for her would also suppress her immune system. Well, that wouldn't work because her immune system was already quite suppressed due to feline leukemia.

So along with Whoopie's twice-daily medications and feeding, I started crushing Orbax and dissolving it in a bit of water in a spoon. When it was thoroughly dissolved, I would suck it up into a needleless syringe and quickly squirt it down Tabitha's throat. Poor dear, she hated that. However, extreme sneezing, labored breathing, and copious mucous secretion all demanded that type of care.

Got the idea? Even if I wanted to sit back and eat chocolates, watch TV, and be good to myself so that I could heal quickly and properly— that wasn't going to happen in this lifetime.

Of course, when I read my emails, I find all kinds of cards from friends admonishing me or assuming that I was already sitting in front of the computer or TV eating chocolates and babying myself.

Oh for Pete's sake. Didn't these people know me by now?

Chapter 3

Mother's Day

Today is Mother's Day, supposedly a day to contemplate the joys of motherhood and maybe get flowers, go out to lunch or dinner, and so on. Well, no one in this house can look forward to a day with any of those items.

I got up about eight thirty and came into the family room. I started watching CBS Sunday Morning as usual on Sunday mornings. After about fifteen minutes, I started hearing a very loud *woop, woop, woop* sound outside. I noticed my ceiling fans were stopping and then lights went out ... Oh no ... No electricity.

I called Progress Energy and reported no power. The woman who spoke with me asked if I could check the circuit breaker box. I told her that I had a broken leg and couldn't go anywhere.

Well, I could, but the circuit breaker box was well hidden behind mounds of furniture, boxes, and such in my garage. No way in the world could any person get to the box. She told me that someone would be arriving within the hour.

I scurried to put on proper clothes as I was still wearing a flimsy cotton nightgown. I don't use air conditioning, and sleeping in next to nothing is usually what I did.

Then I thought about calling Maurice, my handyman, who was planning on coming over later in the day anyway. I left him a message about the electricity and asked if he could possibly come over earlier as I needed help with the Progress Energy people.

I had no idea when he would get my message, but he arrived at my front door about twenty minutes later. I thanked my knight in shining armor profusely, and the power truck arrived. Maurice spoke with the man. He came back and reported that it was believed that an underground cable had been damaged. Maurice was told that another truck would be sent out with equipment to locate and repair the break in the line.

I begged Maurice to get some hot coffee for me because without coffee in the morning, I'm subhuman. Bless his heart, he went to Dunkin' Donuts and came back with coffee.

Maurice and I set up our coffee and doughnuts on my back porch. We sipped coffee and talked while waiting for the repairman. It seemed to take an inordinate amount of time for them to appear, but once they arrived, Maurice went into the backyard and opened the side gate so they could start searching for the break in the line.

Maurice and I stayed on the porch talking while the men worked. Maybe an hour later, we had power restored.

So essentially from nine thirty in the morning to one thirty that afternoon, I was entertaining three gentlemen on Mother's Day. Again, busy, busy, busy …

No matter how much I wished that my predicament could be a reason to pamper the princess in me, life threw me a curve ball, and off I went in a new direction.

I was grateful for friends such as Maurice who were nice enough to help me. He also brought a Mother's Day card that had cats and dogs inside actually dancing to a little tune about Mother's Day. How sweet was that?

How could I ever think of being sad, bored, or anything else? God was keeping me busy and surrounding me with the unconditional love of all my fur babies and the kindness and friendship of others when I was most in need.

I have no idea how in the world all these fantastic things could be accomplished with a hiss-and-moan attitude. I have learned that cheerfulness spreads more cheerfulness and that joy radiates and comes back to you tenfold. I have learned that through osmosis—all the precious wonderfuls who radiate pure joy and unconditional love and always live in the now.

Chapter 4

The Human-Animal Bond

I visit the dog park five days a week and meet all kinds of people. The one thing they all have in common is that they love and adore their children. I try to strike up conversations with all the proud parents at one time or another. Time and again, I am told a super sweet story about their children. It is so wonderful to see their smiles, hear their stories and their laughter, and know I have met kindred spirits, other souls who love their children more than they do themselves.

I made the acquaintance of a lovely husband and wife with a beautiful young puppy. I met them at the park on various afternoons. The husband and wife were of retirement age, and they brought Sophie into their lives. As one can imagine, Sophie was the center of their existence.

When I first met them, I told them about the Sporn no-pull halter collar. They ordered one for Sophie, and the latest report was that it was working beautifully. Sophie was only thirty-eight pounds, but she was strong. I imagined that her full-grown weight would be about sixty pounds. She had a lovely strong body due to German shepherd being in her background.

The husband was easily over six feet tall and had a very sturdy build. No, I am not trying to be nice by not saying he was obese because he wasn't obese. He was tall, slender, and built with a solid skeleton just as his sweetheart Sophie was. However, he did move quite slowly. In fact, he walked so slowly that a caterpillar could have kept up with him. I respected and admired him, and his wife was quite lovely as well.

She was with him and Sophie on two or three visits to the park, but then, only Sophie and her adoring father had been visiting. He mentioned something about his wife not feeling up to visiting. I got the impression without asking prying questions that she was suffering the effects of her medications; she was ill.

On one visit to the park, Sophie played with my Teddy. Teddy was about fifty pounds, and he was the sweetest and gentlest boy on earth. He adored smaller dogs in particular. Numerous times, I have seen him lie on the ground to facilitate a smaller dog being able to crawl all over him and bite and wrestle with him. Teddy was a chow and German shepherd mix, and Sophie was a German shepherd and Doberman mix.

One day, Teddy had picked up a small branch about three feet long and was walking around proudly carrying it in his mouth. Sophie's father walked out into the center of the playground with Sophie between his legs. She was unsure of herself with rambunctious dogs and in particular large dogs. Because she was unsure, she would gladly sit on the bench beside her father or go underneath the bench, where other dogs could not reach her. She was young and unsure of herself, so her socialization was an important issue for her father.

As he and I talked, Teddy walked by, and I bent over and started petting and loving him. When Sophie ventured in my direction, I lavished her with praise and pets. I was so happy that Teddy walked over slowly with the stick, and I encouraged Sophie to take the opposite end in her mouth. I was delighted when she did just that. I whipped out my cell phone and made a video of Sophie and Teddy walking side by side with the branch between their teeth. Sophie's father asked me if I could email it to his wife; he wanted to share the joy of the moment with her. I replied, "Of course!" and did just that. I said nothing more, and we went back to playing with Sophie and Teddy.

Later, as he and I were walking to the exit with our precious wonderfuls, Sophie's father remarked that their Sporn no-pull halter collar had arrived. He told how it was quite a challenge to get it on a wiggling and happy puppy. I laughed as his comment brought back many memories.

He stated that it worked very well on the walk. I could not have been more pleased as I knew the level of total adoration that existed between him, his wife, and his dear, darling, sweet-as-sugar Sophie.

In all my years of pet sitting, I have continually used this collar for this very reason—safety for the most precious family member or members. I cannot imagine ever having a dog slip out of a collar and becoming lost forever.

As I left the park, I thought about him and his situation with his wife. He seemed to be in his late seventies or early eighties. He didn't speak of any illness, but he walked slowly and deliberately. I wondered, *Why in the world did a person of that age acquire a puppy?* Then the kinder and gentler Nanny Fran thought of all the reasons it was a wonderful idea. This precious dear was giving him and his ill wife something to focus on other than pills, doctors, and diseases. That was huge for them. They were sharing joy 24/7 with Sophie.

I also started to think of Joel Osteen's sermon "Your Life is Your Ministry," and I realized that Sophie was ministering to them and I was ministering to all three. I was there for whatever they might need.

We had exchanged phone numbers when we first met, and I had actually given them a Sporn no-pull halter collar to try out. I had told them that I had been a pet sitter for more than twenty years. Of course, when I would show up at the dog park with seven dogs—three of them mine—they saw with their own eyes the adoration I had for all animals.

I do not know what is ahead, but I will gladly be available to the three of them for whatever they need. I have always been honored to care for God's children, and I felt in my heart that God had extended my caring to the husband and wife as well.

When I get to heaven, I might be surprised to learn that my caring for the animals was indeed the way for me to get to people. In general, I stay away from people for many reasons. However, through my business, I have met the most wonderful, caring, and loving people on earth. I am so grateful that I have been able to meet them.

Chapter 5

Always Nanny Fran

I grew up on a farm in the Midwest. Every day, I had animals to tend to. My grandfather and grandmother took my mother, brother, and me into their home and hearts when I was around six. Back in the day, there were no special programs for child care while the single mother worked. Because that was the case, I was so very lucky to grow up on a farm.

We had beef cattle, pigs, chickens, and foxhounds. My grandfather loved to fox hunt. I adored him and went everywhere I could with him. I was his boy so to speak.

Growing up, I was always outside with the animals. No such thing as obesity in my farming community—it was all fresh air, sunshine, and activity. When I was not doing my chores, I was walking in the woods with my dog, riding my pony, or helping my grandfather in the fields driving the tractor.

In the summers, I detasseled corn; my, oh my, that was a hot, dirty, sweaty job if there ever was one. Purdue University was near me, and they were growing seed corn, and pollination by the wrong corn would have been disastrous. Many high school kids did this to earn money.

I slept upstairs in our two-story farmhouse. The ceiling in my bedroom had approximately five-foot-tall walls around the perimeter, and then the ceiling slanted upward toward the middle of the room. With this construction, my ceiling was quite close to me as I lay in bed. I decided I needed something pleasant to look at.

I began cutting pictures out of magazines. Sometimes, I used the entire page if the image was full-page. All my artwork was photos of cats and dogs taken by skilled photographers.

When I was young, the Sunday newspaper came with *Parade* magazine, which was at least twenty inches by twelve or fourteen inches. I was always cutting out pictures of puppies and kittens that were at least that size and taping them to the ceiling. It comforted me to have them watching over me as I slept.

One might think I had a plethora of animals to hug and love on the farm, and I did, but I still had the need for these pictures in my home above my head. Just think what beauty and tenderness to wake up to each day. I assume I taped those photos to the ceiling because I wasn't allowed to have any animals inside. I didn't think too much about that because no other home in my small farming community allowed animals inside either. Animals were animals, and they were supposed to be outside. End of story—no discussion.

Often, an animal would be injured and my family would say, "Fran, you take care of it. You want to be a vet." I always replied, "I'll just love it." I said I wanted to be a vet so I could live and work with animals. Due to my limited exposure to society, I had never heard of a dog groomer, kennel owner, or pet sitter. I never wanted to be a vet because I had never been good with numbers. I loved geometry, but all other math was impossible for me to understand, and I knew that doctors, vets, and scientists had to have good math skills.

Nonetheless, I learned to diagnose illnesses and act quickly, and I had no aversion to blood. Actually, with decent math skills, I most likely would have been a great vet. Back in the day though, girls were supposed to go to school, graduate, and get married. A few went to college if they had wealthy parents, but I wasn't one of the few.

I got married, moved to Minnesota, and worked as a secretary at the same firm my husband worked for as an electrical engineer. I couldn't wait to get our first home so I could have a dog and cat—in our house.

Right after we moved into our home, my husband and I went to an animal shelter. I picked out the finest $3 dog they had and named him George. The shelter workers projected that he would end up being a large dog because he had large paws, but George never got any bigger than a cocker spaniel. He pretty much looked like a black cocker spaniel.

In the early seventies, women were always attending Tupperware parties, baby showers, wedding showers, and so on. At one of those parties, I heard of a woman who had a few kittens she needed to find homes for, and I of course said I'd take one. I named him Michael, and he looked as if he were a purebred Siamese. He was gorgeous.

After a year or two, I drove to my small hometown in Indiana to visit my family. I did that every spring, when my husband would fly up to Canada to go fishing with friends.

While in my town, I saw a very tiny female beagle running the streets. I asked about her, and all I heard was that the family that had had her had split up; the wife and kids were in town, but the husband had run off to Florida with his girlfriend.

I realized that this precious baby was not a top priority on anyone's agenda, so I put her in my car, and we drove back to St. Paul, Minnesota. That was my first dognapping. Yes, it was the first of several. Remember? Nanny Fran can!

So for many years, our family consisted of George the black cocker spaniel, Amy the beagle, and Michael the blue point Siamese.

Eventually, the entire family ran off to Florida. Yes we did. My husband's father had retired to Clearwater and had started a business. He asked my husband if he would like to join him. I said, "Here we come!"

In 1975, we moved to Florida. We drove two cars. I got Michael and his litter box for the entire journey. I assure you that love had a great deal to do with my ability to tolerate the trip, which took several days with a cat in the car We moved during a blizzard, so the heat was on during the entire trip. Heat makes obnoxious smells a thousand times more obnoxious. Even I must admit that.

But with my can-do attitude and incredible love for this sweet dear, Michael and I made the trip to Florida without a problem. Thank heaven for tranquilizers for Michael; however, whenever I would slow down to toss coins into a toll booth, Michael would let out a yowl. Then when the car got back up to sixty-five, he would lie quietly in his cage. I cannot remember how many toll booths I encountered on the freeway through Wisconsin and the beltway around Chicago, but I certainly was glad to be on a regular highway for the shortest leg of the trip, Chicago to West Point.

Once we got to Florida, I took a job as a secretary at Smith's Industries. It was a British firm that manufactured aviation instrumentation for McDonnell Douglas and Boeing. I worked with thirty engineers, and we all reported to two managers.

Over time, everyone got to know I was an animal lover. I started hearing comments such as, "When I die, I want to come back as your dog."

One manager, who was also from Indiana, told me that I was the only farm girl he knew who had animals inside her house. Geesh! At that time, I thought he was retarded to say such a thing.

So for the next several years, I was a secretary, a real estate broker, and then a medical transcriptionist. At no time did I learn about pet sitters. Groomers were well known, but nothing about grooming animals appealed to me as I had always been around foxhounds, beagles, and mixed-breed dogs. I cannot remember a Westminster Dog Show ever being on the television in my home. We were so poor that if I ever saw for instance a standard poodle, I would think that only rich folks had them as pets. All I associated with specific breeds such as poodles was money, and money was never all that abundant in our home.

All I remember about money while growing up was that we could never afford anything. When I was young, I babysat for families in town to earn some money. In high school, I would sacrifice my lunch hour to sell candy from the candy booth we had. That way, I could eat a candy bar or two for lunch and save my lunch money.

When I was young, I made cotton loop pot holders on a loom and sold them in the grocery store. Yes indeed, the kind grocer, Mr. Dutch Lowther, allowed me to put up a pegboard that had been framed and painted to be attractive, and I would hang potholders two by two on hooks. They cost 25¢ for two. This was back in the mid '50s.

No, I was never asked to care for any other farm family's pets. First of all, most farmers never went on vacation. If they did, they had family members or neighbors to come to feed the cows, pigs, horses, and other animals. Cats were usually barn cats, and dogs were fed good old Purina Dog Chow. No fuss or special care was given to the cats or dogs because the other animals supported the farm.

Besides, cats and dogs were always wandering onto farms because city people were always dumping them out of their cars along country roads. Even then, people didn't value them as I did back then and still do.

Chapter 6

Clearwater, Florida, 1994

Eventually, my life changed for the worse, and I had to make career and life changes. I researched pet sitting, and in 1994, I started my pet-sitting business. I advertised midday dog walking and multiple visits daily for days or weeks, and I eventually offered overnight stays at homes.

After very careful consideration, I came up with the name Never Say Goodbye for my business because the animals would be in their own homes while their families were away. They would have the same food, water, beds, and canine or feline buddies as when the family was home. I told the families that nothing would change in the lives except for who was caring for them. It would be as though they never had to say goodbye. My logical, practical, and business mind came up with that name for that reason.

Years later when I dealt with reincarnation, I learned that we do not ever have to say goodbye because our loved ones always come back to us. In fact, we should say aloha because they will be back. I was totally elated to discover that.

As I cared for all the fur children, I fell in love with each one, and I still do. I have met the most loving, kind, and sweet people through this business. In most cases, each family has had me as their Nanny Fran for the life of their pets, usually twelve to fifteen years. Then there seems to be a year or so hiatus, and then I'd get a call: "Nanny Fran, we got a puppy. You have to come and meet her!"

I am always so happy for them. Pure love, pure joy … what more is there?

But there was the daily drudge of driving to work. I found as most people do that driving to a client's home is not always a piece of cake. During the spring in Clearwater, we have spring breakers visiting nearly through the entire month of March, and we have snowbirds that arrive anytime in the fall and stay through Easter. Our roads are a mess with lots of lost tourists, lots of slow-moving tourists, and roads that appear to be parking lots. And certain roads around baseball fields are clogged as well because several ball teams have spring training here in the Tampa Bay area. Yep, can't forget about all the baseball fans.

I mention the clogged roadways for only one reason—scheduling. Pet sitters often have animals that need medications administered two or three times daily at regular intervals. Others need insulin shots for diabetes or phenobarbital administered in a timely fashion to prevent seizures. All my other pet-sitting clients take a back seat when I'm making my rounds because the ones needing medications absolutely have to have priority. Medications needed twice or three times daily are absolute musts.

Geesh, I live here and never go to the beach. My English and Irish fair skin burns in minutes in the sun and wind. I also have Choctaw Indian blood, but that seems to have taken a back seat in regard to melanin. It's not an important issue for me as I'm not someone who sits still for long. I don't fish; I get seasick on a boat. I'm a total landlubber.

Being a total animal lover, I'm doing what I love in a wonderful, warm, and sunny climate year-round. Pet sitters up north deserve the Purple Heart for all the ice, snow, and freezing temperatures they have to contend with in the winter. God bless them!

I remember reading a question nearly twenty years ago in the Pet Sitters International's newsletter: "Can I charge extra for the visit to the home when I need to shovel out the driveway to get to the home?" I say not only yes but hell yes! Most people would wonder why this was even a question. Based on my experience, I say that most people who become pet sitters fall in love with the animals and do anything required to care for them properly.

Pet Sitters International is a worldwide organization that gives out a Pet Sitter of the Year award. These fantastic people are ferreted out from the thousands of pet sitters worldwide by the clients who use their services. One of my clients encouraged me to pass out the organization's nomination forms to my clients so they could nominate an exemplary pet sitter. At first, I thought, *Aw gosh, no. I don't want to ask people to speak kindly of me.*

Well, she persisted. She was appreciative of my services and submitted her application detailing how I had sandbagged her home to keep rising floodwaters from entering. Yes, I had. She was in Europe on a business trip, and her kitties and bunnies were all alone in her two-story home. The waters could easily have flooded the first floor, and I certainly didn't want that to happen. I made several trips to a location where the county provided sand and bags for homeowners to fill and take home. I filled ten bags and made a second trip for ten more. The county put limits on the number you could take with you at one time. I arrange them at her house to prevent floodwater from entering her home. Thank heaven I was successful. This Indiana farm kid had lifted bales of hay and worked in the fields with her grandfather, so that task was not overwhelming for me. The most wonderful part was having peace of mind knowing that her babies were safe and dry.

Several of my families nominated me, and I was chosen one of the top-five finalists for Pet Sitter of the Year in 1999 by Pet Sitters International out of a field of 3,000 pet sitters worldwide. Yes, I was proud of that. I was also very humbled. Afterward, I read several of the letters my clients had submitted. Their letters were so sweet and kind in their description of me that I was reduced to tears.

One family swore that I had even saved their beautiful Cali's life with my love and encouragement of him to eat. He was a red Doberman pinscher, a beautiful soul. Prior to their locating to this area, his family had boarded him at a facility on the other coast. Daily calls to the facility assured them that all was fine. However, when they arrived at the facility to bring him home, he was in terrible shape. It was then that the people caring for him told the family that he hadn't eaten for days. He refused everything, even their homemade chicken soup that someone had brought for him.

When they asked me to visit their home several times daily and care for him, I was certainly honored. I told the family that I would do anything to get Cali to eat and stay well. I even joked that I would dance naked for him if that would get him to eat. Well of course, he and I loved each other, and he knew he was adored. My visits are never short; many times, I have spent an hour or two or even more if my schedule allowed.

I have the most wonderful photo of Cali that I took on a cold winter day. He had a medical condition that didn't allow him to maintain his body heat properly. I put a lovely warm sweatshirt on him and took him out to tinkle and poo. He looked so regal in that white sweatshirt. I would take him in my Jeep Grand Cherokee to a park so we could walk and enjoy nature. He sat next to me on the center console. He was my copilot, and he sat like a king at least a full head higher than me. Imagine the looks I got from other drivers and pedestrians when they saw him. I delighted in watching their expressions. He was my sweetheart, baby, and best friend.

Many families don't value their babies as you or I do, and they don't want to pay a decent wage to an animal caregiver. They hire them because animal caregivers are cheaper than boarding the animals or because they couldn't get a friend or family member to care for them for free.

Most people have no idea of the amount of dedication, common sense, and knowledge of animal care, home security, personal integrity, dependability, and other matters that is involved in caring for a home and the animals in residence. Many people compute the cost of travel, hotel, food, and tickets to Disney but leave out the cost of animal care. Many people are willing to spend money on themselves, but on a pet sitter? Aw, come on. Anybody can walk a dog. Not!

Really now. That's all there is to it?

I could write volumes about dog walking, but suffice it to say that in twenty six years, I have backed down attacking dogs at least a dozen times. Yes, in lovely residential neighborhoods such as yours. Each time, I handled the situation in such a way that the attacking dog turned and walked away, and not one dog or I was bitten, attacked, or harmed in any way. Yes, I turned away an assault on your sweetheart and myself with nothing but my canine understanding and knowledge. A five-five woman with no pepper spray, no stick, no gun, nothing but my iron will and an incredibly calm and confident demeanor diffused such situations time and again. So don't waste your breath telling me that anyone can walk a dog.

My heart goes out to all pet sitters who have not raised their rates for people over many, many years. During that same time, the cost of car insurance, gas, car repairs, and other costs have risen but not the initial fee quoted five, ten, or fifteen years prior. Wrong!

One might ask why a pet sitter would not raise his or her rates. The most common reason is that they love the animals. The owners might be so cheap that they request only one visit per day. However, due to the age and needs of the animals, a pet sitter might make two visits and not inform the client because all pet sitters know that there are people who would visit only once a day and the poor animal would suffer.

Not all pet sitters love and adore the animals more than they do themselves. How would the animal suffer? Maybe the animal cannot hold its urine or feces for twenty-four hours; most cannot. Then if there's an accident in the home, the pet sitter might not see it or clean it up. When the family comes home to a nasty mess, they may decide to get rid of this incontinent or old animal.

Some pet sitters stay only fifteen minutes if that is what they said they would do; a poor animal that needs more attention and care doesn't receive it. Unfortunately, clients might not understand the habits or needs of their precious ones because they have twenty-four-hour access to the backyard courtesy of a doggie door.

I regret to say that many times, people have such busy lives that they do not notice signs of illness, lethargy, or increased water intake in their pets. There are many other things I could mention as well. They don't have a clue as to what their animals need in terms of care.

So here come cheap pet sitters who fly in and out without noting whether the animals are eating, drinking, urinating, and defecating properly. They also have not surveyed the premises to find that the animals had an accident in the home or that the animals got into the trash and ate something harmful. I could go on and on. When you're cheap, you get what you pay for. Unfortunately, the animal pays the price one way or another, many times with its life.

I have found over the years that I am a savior, an angel whenever an animal needs subcutaneous fluids or other special handling and care because of illness. I have also found that once the animal no longer needs subcutaneous fluids or other special care, I no longer hear from the family. You see, if an animal is healthy, the neighbor or friend is free and I charge a fee.

I put it out of my mind that due to my twenty years of experience 24/7 for 365 days a year, I have earned my stripes but am nonetheless not appreciated. What a client who requests the kid next door to care for their animals is saying to me is, "If oops happens to my puppy, all would be forgiven because after all, the kid is only ten or twelve. Or they like their neighbors and don't want to start World War III over an animal dying or running away. After all, it is only an animal, isn't it?

Home security is a major concern. I have never had any advertising on my vehicle for twenty years; I don't want to advertise that my clients are out of town and I'm only visiting their homes three times daily to walk their dogs. No indeed. Anyone canvassing a neighborhood for a burglary could see my vehicle sitting in their driveways.

They would see me walk your tiny Yorkie, Maltese, or Cocker Spaniel around the block, not a Neapolitan Mastiff or Great Dane mind you, and think, *I'll break in when the pet sitter is not visiting and steal the Yorkie along with other belongings or shut it in a room while I raid the premises.*

Whenever I have encountered someone while walking a dog and am asked about the family being away, I say that I'm the mother or aunt. I let them think I'm currently living in the home. I want every person I might encounter to think I live there. I have no idea who that person may be. They could be scouting the neighborhood for a home to break into or an animal to steal.

Chapter 7

Time Is Money—Speed Is Money Too

Cash flies out the window when you speed to any assignment. Yes it does. Tickets are very costly, and you aren't charging enough to pay for a moving violation. Also, you need to be a safe driver. Any fender bender or worse is time consuming.

You have a schedule to keep, so you cannot be late to a home. Many animals are on medications that need to be administered at certain times of the day. If you get in an accident, you'll waste time getting it sorted out and getting a rental; you'll fall ridiculously way behind in your schedule. Besides, you'll have to pay for the rental.

You might say, "Oh no, not me. My husband (boyfriend, neighbor, son, or daughter) will come and get me." Okay, but can you use their vehicles for the rest of the day or next several days while your car is being repaired? You might have an accident at seven in the morning, three in the afternoon, or nine at night. All of the saviors mentioned above might be at work, sleeping, or out of town. You can't depend on someone else to save your bacon.

I strongly recommend becoming an AAA member. One time, I had a flat tire at ten at night; I had to have my vehicle towed to a garage so it could be fixed in the morning. I had to call a taxi to get home and then again in the morning to get to the garage. I was a single woman living alone and had no family to call on. At ten at night, I was not about to call any friends who most likely were either in bed or getting ready to crawl into bed because of work the next morning.

After a few months of accommodating everyone's schedules seven days a week, early morning, late at night, and in the middle of the day, you realize that you have no life. However, you have the best life! Everywhere you go, you are adored. Yes indeed, adored!

Every client of mine knows that there's nothing I wouldn't do for my animals that I wouldn't do for their animals. I always tell clients, "When I'm your pet sitter, your children are my grandchildren." No, that's not a syrupy sweet advertising gimmick; it's the truth. All the animals in the world are my children. Sound funny to you? Not me. God instructs us to care for all the animals, and I'm doing only what he asked.

Yes, I'm the same person you have seen stop my car and make all other traffic stop so I can pick up a turtle and carry it to safety across the roadway. Yep, the same one.

Also, I have stopped traffic by waving to all behind me to stop. Yes, there was a gaggle of geese crossing the road, or a mother duckling crossing with a dozen babies trailing behind her, on and on.

And yes, you'll see me in the future doing exactly the same.

Chapter 8

Dear, Precious Names

I'll confess some silly stuff—funny names such as Fluffer Nuffer Puffer Stuffer, Sweety Weety Neetykins, Precious Wonderfulkins, and Paddy My Boy, my Irish shepherd. Of course he's an Australian shepherd, but since I'm mostly Irish, he's also Irish.

I know that animals know exactly what we're thinking, so I never try to put anything over on them. If I tried and they became aware of that, I'd no longer be trustworthy in their eyes. I could not bear that.

I also tell each animal at some point, "I love you forever and eighty-two more forevers!" I also tell them another thing that most people would find totally stupid, inane, and silly, but it's important for me to say.

Let's say I'm caring for a dog named Mercedes and her family's last name is Miller. I'll sit, hold her beautiful face in my hands, look her squarely in the eyes, and say, "I've met all the Mercedes Millers in this world, and you are the best!" Words of encouragement cannot be heard too often by any creature with a heartbeat.

Sometimes, the animal is in the home for the children, but otherwise, the poor dear is pretty much ignored by the adults there. It is so sad to witness this scenario, but I have witnessed it several times in my twenty-plus years of being a pet sitter.

I have taken dogs to the dog park regularly and have met awesome people with their spectacular dogs. Many times, people have told me that their dog was spoiled. I always replied, "You can't spoil an angel." Of course we can't. And they are angels. They're a million times better than any human I have met in my seventy-three years.

Pure love, pure joy … that is definitely an angel!

I believe that all animals were put on earth to help us along our life paths. Animals offer unconditional love 24/7. Some people are waking up and pairing animals with people who need emotional support to stay well. We all are aware of animals trained to be 24/7 companions for people with PTSD, but I contend that each person has PTSD. The severity per person can vary, but animals always heal whatever the degree of need happens to be.

I have PTSD from verbal abuse encountered in the first twenty years of my life. Then of course, every day, strangers harshly judge and criticize others unjustly. These angels are needed more than ever in our stress-filled and hate-filled society.

Chapter 9

Warm Waterfall of Pure Love

Many of you may wonder how and why I became a pet sitter. Lots of people love animals but don't become pet sitters, groomers, or veterinarians.

I've always loved animals, but it wasn't until I was in my forties that I had to change my life for the better. I had been married to the love of my life for fourteen years, but he was a verbal abuser, and nothing I said or did changed the day-to-day existence of walking on egg shells. Eventually, I felt that my soul was being pulled out of me, and I knew that shortly I would no longer exist if I did nothing about my situation.

At the time I made this decision, I had been working from home doing medical transcription for hospitals. Unfortunately, working from home made me a constant target for verbal abuse from my husband. This was exacerbated when his company did some downsizing and he was let go. He was then home 24/7 with me. He was so abusive that I started typing at night and sleeping during the day to avoid him.

The arrows and rocks hit my heart and were crushing my soul. Eventually, I decided I had to make a change. I was burned out with medical transcription. Depressing as hell! You know, sickness, meds—yuck.

I have always had excellent health and do not like doctors or poisons from big pharma. This was totally foreign territory for me to walk in anyway. I did this only so I could work from home and be with my animals. I also can type faster than most people can speak and have always been excellent with vocabulary courtesy of the two years of Latin I had in high school.

I cannot remember where or how I heard about pet sitting, but when I did, I contacted Pet Sitters International. I became a member so I could learn everything I needed to know. The first thing I did was to purchase Patti Moran's book on how to start a pet sitting business, a great resource. But I learned that setting up your business is only 1 percent of what you need to know to have a successful business.

When I say successful, I'm not talking about many dollars flowing into your hands but about having clients who love you, adore you, trust you with their sweethearts, and trust that you'll come and go when you promise to be there for them and their babies.

After twenty-plus years, I can assure you that many of my clients have had me for their pet sitter for almost fifteen to twenty years and/or the lifetime of their sweethearts. Now that's my definition of success.

Many people have asked me how many clients I have. My reply is always the same; I say that I don't know because actually counting them isn't important to me. The only important thing to me is that when I look at my schedule, I see the same families over and over. That's the mark of a successful pet sitter.

In the first year or so of business, I joined a pet sitters' group that had monthly luncheons. At first, I was thrilled to be a part of this group. I was always sharing new ideas and new forms I had created for client information and so on. That was until one day I realized something—I wasn't like the others in the group.

Others in the group were happily married and were not doing pet sitting to escape into new lives away from their spouses as I was. I realized that most of the lovely young women in the group had children, so this was a part-time endeavor for them. I also came to realize I should not put my questions about the business up for discussion for the same reasons.

My views on any issues were always based on one fact—I was going to do this 24/7 for the rest of my life. None of these women had that goal in mind, so their views would have differed greatly from mine. I learned to trust my judgment and not seek others' opinions. That might sound quite arrogant and pompous, but I knew that I loved and adored all animals. This was not a contest; I was not competing with any other person. I simply wanted to be the best pet sitter in the world.

I began marketing myself, and I persevered for days, weeks, and months, but at times, I became very discouraged. I discovered that many people didn't regard my chosen life work as anything valuable.

One time when I was getting my oil changed, I exchanged business cards with another customer. He read my card, looked me square in the eyes, and asked, "You pick up dog shit and people actually pay you?"

I saw in his eyes that he was thinking, *If she had one more brain cell, she would have a real job.* I was amazed at his response then, but I have come to understand that many people do not value animals as intelligent beings and therefore do not value the services an animal caregiver performs. That was my first ah ha! moment.

My second ah ha! moment came when I visited a client who valued me and my services. When I approached her home, the front door was open. I saw her standing inside the home talking on the phone. She saw me and motioned me in. Her dogs came running to me, and I sat on the floor and hugged and petted them while my client finished her call.

She greeted me and said, "I love my dogs, but you love all animals." That was not an outrageous or unkind statement, but it blew me away. I must have been the most unaware person on the planet. I was in my early forties and had just realized something incredible.

Before I heard her comment, I had thought that those who loved one animal loved all animals. Why not? I thought that was the way God made people. I thought love was love was love. I was blown away to realize that not all people were like me. Well of course not all people; I'm referring just to people who loved animals. I'm not kidding you. Her comment blew me away! How could this even be possible?

I have thought about this, and the only thing I can equate it with is the love of children. Many people have children and love them with all their heart, but they may not be able to stand another person's child for even a minute. I do not mean that these people are mean, evil, or would do harm to any child; it's just that they love only their own offspring. People never cease to amaze me.

I had said that my startup was painful. People asked me if I had ever been a vet tech, vet, and so on. My answer was no. I had grown up on the farm and loved animals. Of course, most people had no idea how much I loved all animals and still do. If someone would want an answer, it would be twofold: animals have always been there for me 24/7 while people have not, and animals have never uttered unkind words with the intent of hurting my soul.

It was definitely hard trying to sell myself. Obviously, people thought that they loved animals and that was why they had one or two in their homes. I can understand how they defined me. I persevered because I needed to get this business started so I could leave my abusive husband and save my soul or what was left of it.

One time, I was driving and feeling quite despondent over the fact that my startup was not starting up very quickly. I guess I was beginning to wonder if my idea had been the greatest idea I had ever generated. I was driving on the street that ran in front of the Humane Society of North Pinellas when I asked, "Dear God, am I doing the right thing by trying to start this business?"

His response was immediate. I felt a flow, a river that ran over and through my body. It was a very warm waterfall of love that entered the top of my head and flowed downward through my entire body and out the soles of my feet. It was a flow of pure love that was very warm and incredibly soothing. I have never experienced anything like that in my life except for that moment. Believe me, he got my attention, and I was impressed. My response was, "I'll take that as a yes!"

Chapter 10

And Years Later ...

Okay, I promise that I will fill you in the past twenty-plus years. In year one, I was still pretty darn clueless. I was so excited to have even one family believe in me and trust me with the care of their sweethearts that I was floating around Pinellas County like a butterfly in my glory. Me! I was walking someone else's precious wonderful. Yes, me! I was incredibly honored to have this angel in my care.

One time, I was walking on a lovely sunny morning with a beautiful sweetheart on a leash. I have always loved nature, so I was soaking in the sunshine, the green of the grass, the lovely trees, on and on. I was in such a blissful state that as I approached a driveway that had a newspaper lying on it, I picked it up and threw it by the front door. Then I nearly floated along the sidewalk with this precious puppy beside me in a state of unmitigated joy. Yes, I did!

I was in such a state of bliss that I noticed a car approaching on the street next to us. At that time in the morning, it was usually someone driving to work. Of course, the driver didn't see me and the beautiful angel by my side, but I thought, *I'm sure he thinks this is the most precious dog he's ever seen.* Wow. Euphoria to the max.

I cannot remember feeling any more bliss than when I was in the dentist's chair inhaling nitrous oxide. Totally true. One time while I was in the dentist's chair, I was under the influence and was dreaming. Remember now that I am not and never have been great with numbers. My vision was $E = mc^2$ *Wow, that's so simple! I get it now!* Yes, I was that euphoric walking a precious fur baby!

Over the years, I've been told many times, "Nanny Fran, you're a bit over the top." Geesh, if they had only known about those incidences. Every time I hear that comment I always think, *I am sorry that you are not!*

For many years, I could not even conceive of doing anything other than visiting homes and loving and caring for the animals inside. Sure, the hours were crazy and the requests for care came at any hour of the day. Some people arranged care months in advance while others did so with only a few hours' notice.

I began to say that my life would change with the next phone call, and it did. I never make plans to do anything for myself without knowing that everything in my life is subject to change. I have told people for many years that I am so flexible that I am Gumby indeed!

Chapter 11

Over the Years

Over the years, I have discovered that from time to time, I have hated this business and resented all the time it has taken me away from my own fur children. As much as I love and adore this business, at times, it's hard for me to leave them and care for other fur children.

One of the hardest times is when I have an ill animal in my home. I cannot fathom how mothers go to work every day and leave their children when they aren't feeling well. My heart goes out to them.

When you have to say goodbye to one of your babies, you can start hating this business because your beloved is gone forever and you think of all the time you spent with other people's fur children. You then resent them and all the time they took you away from your baby. I suppose this is a natural stage of grief every pet sitter goes through.

But I would never change the amount of time, love, and care I give to each family's children. They're alone with the exception of my visits, and they need love and attention along with food, a walk, and maybe medications. Of course I would not shortchange any client's sweetheart on my time and affection for them.

But I do have to confess that every time I do lose one of my sweethearts, I go through that process of hating the business because of all the hours it took me away from my own children.

Chapter 12

Rules Carved in Stone

On a lighter note, I have a few mantras.

1. Never pass up a chance to pee.
2. Always undo the bottom latch on a dog crate first.
3. Always have a spoon in your car.
4. Never wear good clothes to walk a dog.

You realize how important number 1 is after you've started walking your dog and realize that you need to urinate. Along the way, the dog tinkles numerous times on every tree and bush. There you're standing with your legs crossed because every time he or she urinates, your urge to do the same becomes stronger. Unfortunately, you cannot hide behind a bush and urinate. However, if you're dog walking in dense woods, you may be able to get by with that.

Number 2 is a matter of self-preservation, and it applies to large and medium-sized dog crates. Once you have bent over to undo the bottom latch after having undone the top latch, the dog will barrel out and the door will bash you in the head. I think everyone learns that the hard way.

Number 3 is a lifesaver. Each morning, I feed the troops in my home while drinking coffee. Then I hit the road with my thermos of coffee, and after a few stops, I get hunger pangs. I have always said that it's a shame I've never developed a taste for dog or cat food because that is constantly available. However, you rush through traffic to get to each baby and care for them without a thought of your own stomach. Then you hear *growl, growl,* and you feel pain.

Pet sitters might start out in the morning all clean and nice, but usually, maybe as early as lunchtime, they've spilled their coffee on their clothes as they drove around town. Or a sweetheart who adores them has jumped on them with muddy paws and their clothes are now totally trashed. This is the usual for pet sitters. With your clothes all trashed, you don't feel like walking into a restaurant and sitting down to a lovely salad. You know you'll be surrounded by all kinds of people in spotless business attire and wearing makeup and jewelry, which cannot be said of you.

Besides, who has the time to waste an hour or so in the middle of the day? Most days, you're trying to walk dogs before the intense midday heat. You also want to avoid the typical afternoon showers that we can typically tell time by—four in the afternoon always! Or you need to get to a home to administer medications to an animal. You have a schedule and not the luxury of ever telephoning the client's home to say, "Hey, can we reschedule our meeting time? I'm running late today." Dogs and cats don't answer phones.

Of course you could drive through a fast-food place, but I don't recommend that. I haven't had a fast-food meal for over twenty-six years, and never expect to have one before I leave this earth. My body is not a toxic waste dump. Yes, I used to eat double cheeseburgers with all the fixings. Many years prior to my pet sitting, maybe in the early '70s, I was at the Pinnacle Peak, a restaurant in Arizona, and I was served a two-pound sirloin steak. Yes, I ate one all by myself. Of course I couldn't eat the attendant salad, potatoes, or dessert, but I did eat two pounds of steak. The early '70s was a long time ago!

I am not a vegetarian, but I am very close to being one. About the only protein in my life now is ice cream as a meal or dessert, grated cheese, and hard-boiled eggs on my organic spinach salads. My salads also have green peppers, onions, mushrooms, raw broccoli, raisins, and walnuts, so it is indeed a nutritious meal. I used to find time for the salads; today, I fried two eggs and put them between two slices of bread. Breakfast and lunch together. Usually I start drinking coffee the second my eyes open and then proceed to care for my children before leaving for the day. Then usually around 4 in the afternoon I feel hungry. Then it is time for ice cream! I rarely cook as my schedule is so crazy.

Many times when I have had some downtime, I've thought of cooking a casserole or something I could eat on for several days. Then I'd get busy and the food would spoil before I had a chance to prepare the dish. However, I have also found that having made a casserole that serves 8 or more becomes quite tiresome to the palate at the end of the week.

When I was a young homemaker—yeah, what an ancient term—I used to have people over for dinner. I loved preparing new dishes. I loved sitting down with several cookbooks and reading recipes, which I could taste as I read the ingredients. I loved sitting down with a cup of coffee and reading recipes deciding on a salad, entrée, side dishes, and dessert I'd serve to my guests. I found it to be enjoyable and relaxing. I had nearly every cooking implement needed or imagined. Martha Stewart and Betty Crocker had nothing on me. But for years now, finding time to sit and read anything for any length of time takes a power outage in my home, and sometimes even then, I'm not sitting and relaxing for long.

I have collected old rocking chairs. I would refinish them and marvel at the workmanship of the ancient artisans. I always wished the chairs could tell me the history of the people who sat in them and rocked numerous babies. What stories I would hear. Now, I look at my rocking chairs and think one thing. Every chair represents wishful thinking—I wish I had time to relax in them. At least fifty years ago, I spoke with a young woman in an airport. During our brief chat, she said, "I bet you never take a bath in a bathtub. I bet you always shower." I told her she was right. I still am a shower person. In five minutes, I'm out of there and toweling off.

My husband once asked me if I ever sat down. He asked only because he was watching football and I was doing laundry, vacuuming, cooking, gardening, caring for my animals, and handling other tasks. My flybys were interrupting his concentrating on the games, or he was feeling guilty for sitting on his butt and not helping me. I believe he was too lazy to lift a finger and the guilt syndrome never, never entered his mind.

I sometimes will grab some cookies to take along with me in the car to eat with my coffee, or better yet, a jar of peanut butter and some celery and carrot sticks to eat while driving. Nuts are fine too if they don't collect under your partial plate or denture and cause you pain.

Ninety-nine percent of the time, I'll stop at the grocery store and buy some Ben & Jerry's, Graeter's, or Haagen-Dazs and use that lovely spoon I mentioned that I brought from home—metal, not flimsy, breakable plastic. Ben and Jerry's Cookies & Cream Cheesecake is my favorite.

In Florida, we have ninety-plus temperatures from May through October, so even with the air conditioning in your car running, the ice cream is refreshing and nourishing. Besides, trying to eat a sandwich while driving usually results in lettuce, onion, catsup, and mayo falling onto your chest or lap.

I share here something I took great delight in. I was in the beauty shop getting a haircut. Lisa, my hairdresser and dear friend, uses a hearing aid, so I tend to speak a bit louder to her particularly when the hair dryers are going. For many years, I would stop in this shop once a month to catch up with my friend's family and friends and get a haircut. Multiple times over the years there, I heard women talk about this or that new diet they'd discovered. Since I was running constantly and never had time to sit down and munch away to the point of obesity, I was steamed when I overheard these conversations. I always thought, *If you'd just get up off your behind and move, you wouldn't have a weight problem.*

One day, I had had enough and spoke to my friend in a voice loud enough for everyone in the shop to hear. "Lisa, I just discovered that a container of Ben & Jerry's fits perfectly in the cup holder of my center console. Now I can drive down the highway with one hand on the wheel and the other scooping delicious ice cream into my mouth!"

Of course I spoke with great exuberance and delight just to drive home my irritating comment. It was amazing. I could have heard a pin drop; I swear on a stack of Bibles that I felt the air pressure in the shop drop. I felt so darn good after saying that. Yes, the devil came out in me that time. In all my years of never having enough time to sit down and overindulge in a sumptuous repast, at that moment, my bottled-up emotions poured out in those two sentences. Geesh, that felt great.

Number 4 is never wear good clothes to walk dogs. Basically, muddy paws will trash your clothes every time you look at a dog. Beyond that admonition, I say that you should never take good-quality jackets, raincoats, umbrellas, dog leashes, and so on with you on your visits. Millions of times, I've taken off jackets in someone's house and left them there. I don't realize that until the next cool day, and maybe I remember where I left it, or maybe I don't. All I know for sure is that no one has ever called me to say, "Francene, you left your jacket here." Not ONE person! And this is over twenty-six years! Maybe it was a raincoat I took off inside the home, and when I left the home, it wasn't raining. So understandably, I easily forgot I had worn it inside and had left it.

Also, I have left special collars I use for dog walking. I get engrossed in the care of the animals, writing notes for the family about our time together, refilling water and food bowls, giving medications, and so on, and then I walk out without the collars.

By the way, this note-writing comment is true. Unless I'm doing daily dog walking five days a week, I write notes. My dog-walking clients get text messages telling them if their baby pooed and tinkled or ate something off the ground as we walked and I had no idea what it could have been, or he or she was happy, sad, or spunky and sparkling as opposed to lethargic and acting as though he or she didn't feel well. That is midday dog walking. Otherwise, I might actually talk with a client frequently about his or her home and baby or write about our adventures that day.

This note writing can intimidate some pet sitters. Many years ago, I had three women working with me. All seemed to have excellent communication skills, but one couldn't spell or write well. In fact, she reacted as though she had been impaled on a stake when I asked her about leaving notes for the clients. I would stop by the home of the clients she handled while the client was away and write notes myself. That was also an opportunity to double-check on the fur babies to make sure all was well. After all, my name and reputation was on the line if a client was dissatisfied about the quality of the visits.

Again, back to equipment used daily—your equipment and clothing. The collars I have used for twenty years are very special collars; they cost $20 each, but people never call to tell me that I left them there. I interject here that unless that particular client is using the same type of collar on his or her dog, mine would stand out like a sore thumb to them.

The most I have ever gotten is a call to book me for pet sitting again, and maybe then the client will mention that I left collars the last time I visited. Many times, that last visit was six months or a year earlier. Like I couldn't have used them in the interim? Or maybe I was racking my brain trying to remember in which home I might have left them?

And never has anyone mentioned the jacket I left there six months earlier. Okay, I understand. The home has several occupants, and each family member has more than one jacket, so mine got lost in the shuffle. However, I never got it back. So don't wear good clothing to pet sit.

Chapter 13

Social Skills

This area is super important—speak well. Use proper grammar. Don't use slang. People don't want to think they are entrusting their homes and animals to someone who's not educated or bright. Don't be offended; great speaking and writing skills will get you far in regard to impressing homeowners interviewing you.

You are there aspiring to be the majordomo of the manse. Yes, you will be in charge of everything. Your credentials need to be impeccable. Home security is the first and foremost issue. You think of yourself as an animal care specialist, but you're aspiring to be as well the best home security specialist in the world.

If a home is secure, the animals inside will be safe. Without that, no one cares if you are the best pet sitter, dog whisperer, dog trainer, and so on.

For five years, I wrote a monthly newspaper column, "Ask Nanny Fran." Time and again, when interviewing potential clients, I would hand them copies of the newspaper, and the expressions on their faces would speak volumes, *She's smart. She's a newspaper columnist!*

No matter what my credentials or abilities might have been, the simple matter that I was an animal caregiver meant to many that I must not have been very bright or well educated. I've had people ask me if I had a real job. My Lord, people don't think before they speak.

I delight in telling about an experience that would make a person wet their underwear and changing the wording to: Now that would make you tinkle in your frillies!!! I always get gales of laughter.

Chapter 14

Home Security

My cardinal rule over the years was never have signs on your vehicle advertising your pet-sitting business. I stressed this before, and I stress it again. A pet-sitting sign on a car outside a home means the owners are away, and burglars can spot that as easily as they can newspapers piling up in front of a door.

Most potential clients don't give this cardinal rule of mine any thought until I describe how advertising on a vehicle is an engraved invitation to any and all burglars. That is the first point you need to make to leave a good impression with a potential client. They might believe that the most important asset you can present is your love of animals and your knowledge regarding veterinary first aid. Set the record straight; it will be your record, not that of the kid next door, not another pet-sitting organization, but you. In this business, each assignment is critical. You won't be asked to come back to care for the precious wee ones if you screw up your first assignment with them.

I've found that once people get to know you, they will like you enough to trust you inside their homes and trust that you'll visit their homes as requested. People will see that you love their children and that they are comfortable with you. People will realize you have common sense and can address serious issues regarding their pets' health and wellness by taking the pet to the best twenty-four-hour animal emergency hospital after hours and to their vets when the animal has a medical issue. When all of this is in place, you'll have this client forever.

I have had many clients for over twenty years. Steady clients are angels who will serve as great references particularly if they've been your clients for years and years. Your potential new clients who got that earful of wonderfulness will be delighted to have met you.

I stress the importance of not sharing your duties with neighbors, family members, friends, and so on who are not pet-care professionals. These people can leave doors open and lose pets. They can also do other things inside the home such as break or take objects, drink the alcohol in the home, or look through the client's mail (family members especially). Such substitutes, being wonderful neighbors, best friends, or relatives, will blame the breakage or loss on you. Guess whom the homeowner will believe? Not you.

I've had people inform me that so-and-so will be stopping by intermittently to play with Fluffy so Fluffy doesn't get too lonesome. They're saying that they're asking someone to check up on you. They are cynical, nontrusting people who want to make darn sure that you are there. However, who is this person? You as the pet sitter do not know this person and will not be introduced to this person before the pet-sitting assignment commences. You will be in a strange home in a strange neighborhood with a complete stranger possibly walking in on you at any time. For all you know, this supposedly trusted person could be an ax murderer, a serial rapist, whatever … You might want to either turn down such an assignment or voice your concerns for your own safety and security and request a meeting beforehand. If your potential clients have any common sense, they'll understand your logic and agree to a meeting.

Think about it this way. You visit a home, you're killed—who suffers? Your family and animals will have to endure your death, and your clients, who are out of town depending on your visits, might have a cleaning woman come in and find your body. Other than the cleaning woman, who would know?

I am a widow, and I wouldn't be missed at my home except by my starving animals. I have no person who might walk inside and easily figure out that I hadn't been in the home for several days.

Chapter 15

"I love animals! I'd love to be a pet sitter!"

Sounds like fun, doesn't it?

The above comment is one I have heard at least a hundred times.

Please do not think that being in business for any number of years is easy. Most pet sitters go out of business in the first month or so because they do not market themselves properly or they screw up with the clients they sign up … and believe me, word gets around. People tell other people about you, people tell their vets about you, people tell their groomers about you, so don't think that giving less than 100 percent to every client on every visit won't be noticed.

Pet sitters leave the business when their spouses or significant others complain that they never see them. Pet-sitters' spouses will complain when they can't participate in Christmases, Thanksgivings, birthdays, on and on like other families, but holidays are when everyone travels, and that's when people need a pet sitters' services.

Pet care is a great deal of fun when the animals are sweet and loving. It's a great deal of fun when there are no health issues and there are no pills to be dispensed. It's fun and easy when there are no geriatric pets that have to be lifted to a standing position and nearly carried outside to tinkle and poo. Usually in such cases, accidents in the home need to be cleaned up as well.

It's a great deal of fun when an animal loves you and the entire planet; however, many animals are rescued precious wonderfuls that need special handling and lots of wise TLC. I have a home full of rescue animals, and most show no signs of trauma. I've had one dog for six years and another for ten years, and both are petrified of all people except me.

One of my dear ones is fine in her home with her pack, which includes me. However, whenever I need to take her outside, she becomes scared. You may very well have babies such as these to care for, and that will require unlimited patience and kindness.

Do you have the patience, empathy, and understanding of basic canine or feline instinctual behaviors? Will you spend maybe an hour or two trying to earn an animal's trust, or will you rush inside, snap a leash on the dog, run outside for a tinkle, dash back inside to toss some kibble into the food bowl, and leave? What will you have accomplished in ten or fifteen minutes? Nothing. Treating any animal in such a fashion is a horror to me and the owner.

They're paying you for your time. They know that their pet needs human companionship or they will grieve for their owners. They will sometimes even refuse to eat. Yes, some dogs will eat only when someone is in the home. They are termed social eaters. I cannot ever remember a ten- or fifteen-minute visit in my entire twenty-six years.

Rollerblade pet sitting is sickening. I also want to speak up here about a very special issue. When you are walking a pet, loving a pet, refilling and cleaning its food and water dish, be in the moment with that special angel. Have your cell phone turned off. The home and the fur child demand your complete attention. You can check your phone after you're finished and sitting in your car before you drive to your next assignment.

Do not even consider for one minute walking any dog with your ears plugged into your cell phone. This is a precious angel, and you have to be aware of everything surrounding this sweetheart and yourself. Oops will mean nothing if you screw up.

Speaking of spending time, the following mundane issues do take time. Your clients will notice something as simple as vacuuming the carpet, sweeping the floors, leaving a spotless sink, etc. They might not gush all over you with compliments, but they will be calling you the next time they're planning a trip.

Clients do appreciate the small things you do because when they arrive home exhausted from their vacation, business trip, funeral, or wedding trip, they will have so many things to attend to before they can get back into their usual routine, and they'll be grateful that they don't have to deal with the everyday, mundane issues such as the light housekeeping issues I mentioned.

Rest assured that included in those mundane issues is making sure the cat's litter box is spotless. I don't mean simply scooping out the urine clumps and feces; I mean as well sweeping the floor all around and under the box to make sure the area isn't covered in litter. Sometimes, cats will miss the box; if they do, grab paper towels and cleaning fluid and on your knees spray and wipe the area clean, and that includes the bottom of the litter box.

Last but not least, make sure all wastebaskets in the home have fresh liners and all the smelly trash, kitty box cleanup bags, and all the paper towels you used to wipe up the dog and kitty tummy toss-ups are in the trash that is outside waiting for the garbage man. Nothing stinky should be left in the home. You might leave the home at eight in the morning and the family might arrive home at two the following morning. In that time frame, anything and everything can become odiferous in a closed-up home.

With the advent of smart phones our business becomes so much easier and fun. I've videoed pets playing and sent the videos to the clients. How wonderful to actually see Fluffy thoroughly enjoying life as usual while their mother and father are away. I also take my digital SLR camera with me so I can take absolutely fantastic photos of them.

After having taken a few of them, I will have them printed and will leave those gorgeous photosfor the clients to ooh and ah over when they come home. Most people are not good photographers. I started taking photos of people's pets twenty years ago when I noticed the photos on the fridge of Fluffy were awful. Several years down the road when Fluffy runs over the Rainbow Bridge, these photos bad as they are will be used in the grieving process. I think that each person should have beautiful and delightful photos of their furry friends at that painful and sensitive time.

My clients have told me when they've seen my photos, "This *is* Fluffy." They mean to say that I've captured the pure, individual essence of that animal. I am honored because that's my goal when I photograph animals. I never put a stupid hat on the pet and snap a picture. I want to honor the animal, not dishonor or make fun of the dear one. I've also heard, "Fran, my husband has earned his living with photography, and he says your photos are quite good." *Woo hoo!* Such photos are indications of the time and care you've given to clients' precious wonderfuls. I don't pose animals; I just wait until I see a perfect picture, and I have my camera at the ready. Animal photography teaches patience. The only way to get great photos is to wait, watch, and snap at just the right time.

I've had only one person in twenty-six years tell me that she noticed what time of day it was when I took some photos of her children. Yes, Kellianne, you were the only person who ever noticed that. She had requested only one or two visits per day, but I thought the animals needed three. I made three visits because the animals needed that many. I didn't care that the client had requested and paid me for only two visits per day; anything for the animals! The beautiful photos I look at today were certainly worth that extra visit. Besides, I used the extra time to snap a few more great shots.

Chapter 16

Got the Right Stuff?

I'm serious. As a pet sitter, you'll be asked to be totally available and dependable 24/7 and capable of handling any and all situations that may arise. At this point in my life, I feel I could be an excellent EMT. I have no idea how many times in twenty-six years I've had to make a decision in a split second to prevent a disaster or rescue an animal in my care.

Yes, dog walking is ripe with opportunities for disaster. Anyone walking a dog needs to be strong, observant, alert, and quick in any situation. Before pet sitting, I used to play racquetball and tennis. Both are excellent training for learning to move quickly.

You need to be incredibly observant of all of your surroundings. You will develop the most incredible hearing because you'll be straining to hear all kinds of sounds especially the clinking and tinkling of dog tags not coming from the dog you are walking. That noise means there's at least one more dog in the area. Avoid all dogs at all times. Remember, this is not your dog, so never take chances.

When walking in a neighborhood, keep an eye out for any open garage doors or garage doors being opened or gates to any front or backyard that are open. If there's a fence, there's usually a dog. If the dog in residence is out in the yard or in the garage and is territorial, it can charge at you and your dog in a split second. Simply cross the street or turn around and walk back the in direction you came. And consider this—you might be walking a dog that doesn't like other dogs, and you don't want to witness a dogfight.

You have absolutely no control over anything surrounding you and the dog you're walking. Excellent hearing is an absolute must. Your hearing is pitiful compared to your dog's hearing. Your dog for instance can hear the tinkle of another dog's tags several blocks away while you cannot. He is prepared well in advance to attack or greet and possibly play with another dog.

If you come across another dog, you need to assess its body language as well as that of the dog you're walking to determine its interpretation of this meeting. If your gut tells you that this situation could quickly turn into a nasty encounter, make a U turn. The dog you're walking is not yours, but you are totally responsible for its health, safety, and security.

Do what you think is best at all times. I listen to all my clients and their needs, desires, and wishes. But the bottom line is that I will do nothing to endanger an animal.

I referred earlier to the Sporn no-pull halter collar that I use exclusively on every dog I walk. It's the safest and most humane collar ever invented. I've never had a dog slip out of one. Another bonus I get from that collar is the fact that never in twenty-six years have I had a rotator cuff tear (surgery is required to correct this condition) or a lower-back injury. This is important information. You can have several dogs to walk any one day, but you won't be able to if you have an injured shoulder or a lower-back injury. You may not be able to walk dogs for several weeks if you figure in surgery and then time to heal.

I cannot remember how many clients have told me, "Just open the front door and let him out to pee in the front yard. I don't bother with the leash." I tell them that the leash will always be on their dogs before I open the door.

It's all I can do not to say, "If your dog rushes out into the street and is hit and killed by a car, you're telling me that you'll be okay with that?"

Another ability that is essential to pet sitting is familiarity with all the streets in your area. Prior to starting my pet-sitting business, I sold real estate, and that was at a time before laptops, cell phones, and GPS. I relied on paper maps, and I developed an excellent sense of north, south, east, and west. I also got to know housing subdivisions. So when someone would call about pet sitting, I knew whether they could afford my prices as soon as I learned where they lived because I knew the subdivisions' general income level.

Today, if someone asks me for directions, I still tell them to go north on Main and make a left on 33rd. I say, "You'll be going west. On the corner is a Mexican Restaurant. Actually, that's on the northwest corner." At some point, I note their puzzled looks, and they ask me for a street address. That's when I realize they're relying on their smartphones for navigation. How sad. No phone, no go.

I strongly recommend observing your surroundings and knowing your streets so you can evade stalled traffic and a million tourists or spring breakers when needed.

You have to be observant while walking the family dog, but you also have to be a detective on the client's property and inside the home. You need to be a super sleuth, a great detective for the sake of the health, safety, and security of the animals and yourself. Note anything that's been moved or is missing since you first walked into the home. If someone else has been in the home, you need to know about that. Your safety is as important as the safety of the animals in the home.

One paranoid pet sitter told me that she puts a piece of string on the top of the front door and back door; she notes if the string is still in place on the next visit to see if someone has been in the house in the meantime. Anything moved or missing could be a sign of that as well. If anything is broken or stolen you might be blamed for that. So be very observant of any changes inside the home when you come and go several times a day or even once per day. Always be fully aware of the mood and actions of the animals in the home. If they act fearful or timid then you might wonder if someone had visited the home between your scheduled visits. You also need to note if they are eating and drinking normally. A dog might have (and they typically do) raided the kitchen wastebasket. They may have ingested something that made them vomit. Not only will they be acting lethargic or not eating because they are not feeling well but they may have vomited. Be sure to check all rooms for vomit, urine or feces. Make sure that no appliances have been left on in the kitchen or in the bathroom. I have found curling irons and coffeepots left on in homes.

Chapter 17

Do You Want to Become Rich? Become a Pet Sitter!

Person after person has asked me over the years if I made a lot of money pet sitting; they wanted to earn extra income by walking dogs and wondered if there was a great deal of money to be made in the business.

Actually, you can make money in this business if you live in the right area and make the right connections. I recently learned of a pet sitter in Jacksonville, Florida, who does all kinds of pet sitting for the players of a well-known Jacksonville sports team. I've heard of pet sitters in California who make a very good living because of the wealthy people there, but I take into consideration the cost of living in that state—everything's relative.

Well folks, I'll tell you that there isn't a great deal of money in this business no matter how you analyze it. If your job required you to be on call 24/7 all 365 days of the year, it would pay you handsomely and you'd have benefits as well. But that is the time commitment all pet sitters make when they enter this business. Many find it too demanding and call it quits after a few weeks or a month.

From time to time, you might have some greenbacks or a fat check in your pocket, but when you analyze the time spent traveling to and from each home, the time spent with each animal on each assignment, and the cost of gasoline, car maintenance, repairs, and insurance plus sundry other costs that are totally unpredictable, then no, there is no money in pet sitting.

As of this date, my wonderful car that I adore is turning 240,500 miles. My faithful companion has been my trusted transporter for ten years. However, I recently paid $700 for repairs, and now I need $400 to repair my air conditioning. Believe me, it's not fun to drive around town in hundred-degree temperatures, but I'll have to until I can come up with that $400. I also have no home AC because I don't have the money for repairs.

Yes, I want to make those repairs as this vehicle has at least another 50,000 miles on it according to my mechanic. I filled up my tank at Costco, and it cost $60. I had never paid that much for gasoline in ten years! A fill-up used to cost $20 to $30, so $60 is outrageous, and I should note that that's a weekly cost. Remember to figure in repairs, insurance, gasoline, and car payments in the dollar amount you ask your clients per visit.

Most people in our country wouldn't give their employers five minutes of their precious time unless they were paid for those five minutes. Such greed-driven people should never consider pet sitting. If you're considering pet sitting, you need to equate it with child care. These are people's children, and a pet sitter should think of them as such. There's nothing I wouldn't do for an animal. For people? Hell no! That's why I've been doing this for well over twenty years. I prefer the company of animals to the company of people 24/7. I've heard this same comment from animal lovers countless times over the years.

You've heard, "When you're doing the work you love, the days are never long." It's true. Seven days a week for well over twenty years, I've gladly spent my life with animals and don't regret that decision in the least.

Nope, I'm not rich; that's because I've spent thousands on tooth implants. If you don't believe me, go ahead and contact Dr. Mark V. Davis, a specialist in implant and restorative dentistry. He's taken pictures of the miraculous restorations he has performed in my mouth and has asked permission to show these pictures around the world where he has given talks. So my mouth has been around the world without me.

I guarantee that the hardest surface on the planet bar none is the top of a dog's head. Many times, I have bent over to say hello to a dog and it lifts its head to give me a kiss and then *bam!* My two front teeth made contact with the top of the dog's head.

And on more than one occasion, I've been bitten by a cat. No problem until there is a red streak running up my arm toward my torso. Then ER visits and two weeks of an antibiotic, twice daily, all costing dollars—a few hundred here and a few hundred there and I'm fine. One cat bite will easily cost you more than you made at the client's home visiting that cat.

Many years ago, my own cat's bite landed me in the hospital. It was my own fault. He was a biter, but I loved him with all my heart for seventeen years. However, one time, I waited several hours before going to the ER, where I encountered a physician without a clue as to how to treat a cat bite. My God, what an idiot! The next morning, I saw my primary care physician. He took one look at my arm and asked me how long it would take me to get to the hospital.

I got myself hospitalized and ran my business for three days from my hospital bed with my laptop and cell phone while my right hand was suspended over my body and my left arm had an IV in it. I was being given Unisyn (an antibiotic) intravenously every six hours for three days in a row.

The first day in the hospital, I was visited by a young man—my doctor. I inquired why my right hand was suspended in the air.

He replied, "We're hoping to not have to do surgical drainage."

I thanked him and sat there like a good little girl for three days. You betcha. Surgical drainage? No way. My kitty's bite was almost in my wrist joint, and having bacteria in that location can become quite an issue as I found out.

So for three days, Never Say Goodbye Pet Sitting Service was doing business as usual only from a new home base. Cell phone and laptop helped me service every client as needed with the help of two or three helpers. Thank heaven for them.

I always appreciated every person who ever worked with me because the hours in the business were terrible. And, yes, these helpers dealt with pee, poop, vomit, and blood just as I had dealt with all of the above over the years. No, there is no glamour to this job, just lots of loves, kisses, tummy rubs—you get the idea.

I don't love you … I adore you! Yes, that's how I feel about all the animals, and I always have. Unless you feel this way about all animals, you have no business being in this business. They're all angels, and if you're not knowledgeable enough to understand them, you shouldn't be near them. I grew up with animals and lived in the woods, barnyard, and barn most of my childhood. Animals have always loved and adored me, and I have always adored them. I feel so blessed to have had the childhood that I had. I thank God every day that I didn't have to grow up in a concrete jungle.

Chapter 18

Heaven Watches Over Us

As I type this, I have my nearly twenty-year-old kitty, Noodles Elizabeth, lying in front of my computer screen all stretched out and watching me. Maybe she is telepathically sending me information for my book.

Oh my, if she could talk. She's seen so much. She knows where all the bodies are buried. She knows all my strengths and weaknesses. She knows me better than I know myself.

Wow, Noods, it's been a wild ride hasn't it? From 1994 to 2018. In 1994, you were a wee kitten who fit in the palm of my hand. Yes, you and your brother and sister. Your dear sister didn't live more than a few months when it was discovered that she had a congenital defect that could be fixed only by surgery at a fancy university, and the humane society didn't have the funds to pay for that. So after three attempts to bring her back to normal, we all had to say goodbye. Geesh, it was so sad.

Your brother, Boston Blackie, was with us for fourteen years. It was such a surprise when he became ill. He had never once been ill, and then his tummy swelled with fluids. Dr. Marrazzo said that it was cancer and that there was nothing I could do to save him. Those were the hardest words I ever had to hear and deal with.

What do you mean, "There is nothing I can do"? Nanny Fran can, Nanny Fran did, and Nanny Fran accomplished whatever she set out to do! That is Nanny Fran! However, this time, there was nothing I could do.

So here we are, Noods, you and me. I guess we're indestructible. I'm so proud of you. As you have put on the years, you've turned into a magnificent woman who always knows she's the queen of our home. You are a shining example of how to live out the golden years.

And speaking of the golden years, Whoopie is a shining example of a dog showing how to enjoy the golden years. Whoopie is a golden retriever and basset hound mix; she has the body and coloration of a golden and the short legs of a basset hound. I have no idea who named her Whoopie, but she's definitely on this planet to have a good time. She's a real party girl.

When the household is quiet, I'll be sitting here typing or watching TV and Whoopie will stand up, grab a toy in her mouth, and come over to me so I can play with her. What a cheerful and happy girl.

I cherish these days when I can spend time with my children. When I was starting my business, I was on call and on the road constantly driving from house to house. Many nights, I stayed overnight at people's homes with their babies while mine were home alone.

Over the years, I had several of my own children go home, and I was devastated. No matter how much I loved all the children on this planet, at those times, I hated my job. At those times, I would raise my rates because I figured that if I was going to be taken away from my own children, people would pay for my time. No mother or father wants to miss watching her or his children grow up. No one goes to heaven saying, "Gee, I wish I had spent more time at the office." It's always, "I wish I had spent more time with my family, my cherished ones."

God, who is always watching over me, knows when he will call one of his children home. Recently, something happened that I believe was orchestrated from above. I met a lovely man, Luis, at the dog park one afternoon and gave him my card. A few weeks later, I got a phone call from him. He was going in for hip replacement surgery, and he wanted me to meet his dogs. We sat and talked in his apartment, and I got to know his dogs better. He wanted me to take his dogs to my home for three or four nights so they wouldn't be at the apartment alone. I said I would gladly do that.

I visited his apartment the evening before his surgery and gathered his puppies, their toys, food, dog beds, and so on, and we went to my home.

Four days later, Luis got home, and I returned his babies. We talked for quite a while. He looked so good; he could have been the poster boy for hip replacements. There, I met a young woman who was going to start visiting his apartment three times daily to walk his dogs for him because he was using a walker.

A week later, the young woman called and said Luis had returned to the hospital. She hoped I could take his babies in until he returned, and I said I would. I got a call from Dimitri, a longtime friend of Luis's. Dimitri and his wife had known this wonderful man for over thirty years. He told me that sepsis had set in while Luis was in the hospital and that he had suffered several strokes. Dimitri said that Luis was on a ventilator and hadn't regained consciousness. He died shortly after.

Luis was a unique person. We talked about many things on each of my visits, and I sensed that he was a very kind, gentle, and wise person. I had looked forward to getting to know him better.

Dimitri called and asked if I could find homes for Isabelle and Cookie and ideally together. I said of course I would. He invited me to a memorial in honor of Luis. I told him that I very much wanted to attend. That was the first time I had been invited to a memorial service for a client. It was a lovely service in Dimitri's home.

I did indeed learn a great deal more about Luis at the memorial ceremony. Several friends who had known him for a great many years were there. I learned so much about this incredible individual. His life was very interesting, and I was blessed to be invited to his memorial service. The comments and stories I heard made me realize that this man had the kindest heart for animals. I feel that he had seen the same thing in me when we met at the dog park. I believe that he was further convinced that I adored animals as much as he did when I went to his apartment to meet his babies. Dimitri told me that Luis had mentioned to him that his dogs absolutely loved me.

I wonder if Luis was somehow aware that he was going to be going home soon. I believe God guided him to me so that when he did go home, his babies would have a home with me. Whenever I am loving and playing with Cookie and Isabelle, I think of Luis. I hope he is watching over them, me, and all the other children in our home. I can imagine his pure joy in heaven. He's again with all the previous puppies he loved and adored. I envy Luis.

One evening, I went to a street festival in Safety Harbor. I took my Patrick, and we enjoyed walking the streets with other families and their dogs. I was shocked beyond belief when I met a family whom I had not heard from since their beautiful puppy, Chase, had unexpectedly passed away. I nearly did not recognize the husband and wife at first. However, when they mentioned Chase and the fact they still had the beautiful pictures I took of him, I remembered them. Chase was so incredibly beautiful that I had taken some great pictures of him, and I'd had several enlarged. I'd fallen madly in love with this beautiful soul.

We spoke of Chase, and six years later, I still wanted to cry as we talked of him. He was so sweet, kind, smart, and beautiful. I indeed fell in love with him; I fell hard for him. Whenever his picture flashes before me on my computer, I go through all the incredible feelings that I had for him. I feel pure joy when I look at his gorgeous face and smile and then total disembowelment when I think of how he left us in the blink of an eye. He was so young. No one understood what had happened. It was strange that I bumped into these people six years later, when Luis went to heaven and I acquired Isabelle and Cookie.

I have no idea what God is trying to tell me, but I hope I'm doing everything the way he wants me to. God does indeed watch over me. Many times, I do not realize that he is helping me until after the fact.

The other day, I visited a puppy to let him go out to tinkle and have his evening meal. On previous visits, this puppy had stayed in his bedroom and barked at me as though I were a stranger. Knowing that to be his usual behavior, I planned on spending a great deal of time in the home. I walked in talking cheerfully as I said his name and went into the kitchen to prepare his dinner. I put his dinner on his puppy placemat and watched TV until he came out to eat. Eventually, he would remember who I was and warm up to me. That didn't take long.

One day, my schedule was such that I couldn't spend an inordinate amount of time with him. Well, God helped me out. As I was opening his front door, my cell phone started ringing. I answered it once I got inside. Shortly after that, the house alarm went off. That had never happened at this home before. I looked at my cell phone and found a text message from this sweetheart's mother. She said that she had forgotten to turn off the alarm; she gave me the code to turn the alarm off. I did so immediately and then texted her back that the alarm was off and all was well.

The horrible noise of the alarm made her puppy come out of the bedroom and into the living room. How wonderful! I was able to let him outside and then back in for his dinner. We had some cuddle time, and he got a second chance to tinkle before I left.

Several days later, I realized that I had been worrying about this baby staying in his mother's bedroom forever and not coming out to eat. I guess God didn't want me to have to deal with that issue again with this baby, so he had orchestrated the alarm going off. I believe he had given me a helping hand with this puppy.

Here's another occurrence that I believe was orchestrated from above. I have two dogs I visit each weekday for a midday dog walk. One is a Labrador and the other is a beagle. This beagle's name is Pepper. He's known for digging under fences and getting out of his backyard. Only God knows why he insists on doing that.

One morning, I pulled into their driveway and saw Pepper's father escorting Pepper from the neighbor's backyard. He had dug under the fence again. Pepper came over to my car and hopped inside to go to the dog park. I noticed that his harness was about to fall off. Somehow, Pepper had gotten his front feet withdrawn from the harness, which was sitting behind his head. It would have just fallen off the next time he put his head down to sniff the ground. I told Pepper's father about this and suggested that Pepper also wear a regular dog collar with another tag; if he did manage to escape the harness, he would have the collar with identification.

As I was reinserting Pepper's feet into his harness, I noticed a very pungent dog odor coming from the harness. I am pretty much nose blind to all animal odors, so my noticing that tells you how pungent it was. I took him to the dog park, and almost immediately, he started rolling in something extremely stinky. Deer poo, possum poo, armadillo poo—who knew? I put a leash on him and walked him over to the water hose, where I tried to wash off as much stinky brown stuff as I could from his fur and harness. When we arrived back at his home, I wrote a note to his mother detailing his roll in the yucky stuff.

Between that visit and the next, I went to the pet store and got another identification tag made up for him. Suffice it to say that the next day, he smelled very nice and his harness had no odor at all. Mom had bathed him and washed his harness. Then I gave Pepper's family the new identification tag so it could be affixed to a regular collar.

So with God's help, we learned how easily Pepper could slip out of his harness, and that enabled us to put on a regular collar that he could not slip out of and attach a new identification tag. Thank heaven we also got the stinky harness washed.

I have found on several occasions that I am watched over while driving. One time, I was approaching a light that was changing to red. I applied my brakes, but no matter what I did, I was still moving forward. I turned right and left and practically stood on my brakes, and yet I was still going forward.

I mentally must have said *Help!* or *I'm going to crash!* because my car miraculously stopped. I couldn't believe it. I knew for sure that someone had intervened to help me stop.

Another time when I was driving, my life was supernaturally saved again. I was driving a loaner from my car repair shop, a Chevy muscle car, and I loved the power and speed of this vehicle. I was heading home with precious Molly, my dear Cocker Spaniel, on the seat next to me. I was driving on US 19, which is usually a very congested major highway, but it was about eight or nine at night, so rush hour was over. I was driving much too fast and enjoying every minute. I went over the overpass, and on the other side was a stoplight. There were three lanes and a left-turn lane. Two of the three lanes were open, so I planned to fly through with no problem. But a car started to cut across all three lanes to get to the left-turn lane. It seemed that no one saw me; I was about to crash into three cars.

I turned the steering wheel left, right, left, right all the while thinking, *No no no!—I'm not going to crash and die!* I somehow emerged unscathed and continued north with Molly sitting beside me. I realized that somehow, God and angels had intervened. I cannot tell you how they orchestrated my safe passage because everything happened in a few seconds. It was all a blur to me with the exception of remembering that I was absolutely determined to *not* crash and die. I've read of angels orchestrating cars passing through one another and no passengers at all being injured. Believe me, that could have happened in this instance, but I do not know.

I stopped at the next home to take the dog for a walk and tuck him in for the night. Afterward, Molly and I continued toward home.

When I got home, I found my computer man still working in my computer. I told him, "You won't believe what just happened to me." I told him of my desperate avoidance of crashing and dying. I said, "It's one thing when your life is saved and you don't know it, but it's totally another experience when you *do* know that your life was spared."

He told me that I was still white as a ghost. I believed him; I was still feeling stunned by the incident even an hour later. It rarely happens that you know without a doubt that divine intervention saved your life. In this case, it was my life as well as dear Molly's life.

The human man/woman funny part of this story comes from a statement this man had made earlier in the evening. I had met him through a chiropractor; he said that he had been a fireman. He had told me, "My life is pain." My thought was, *Hey buddy, if you're trying to impress me, forget it. I'm not attracted to anyone who is a walking pity party.*

After I told him about my near tragedy, he walked behind the sofa where I was sitting and started massaging my shoulders. I couldn't help it … I jumped up as if I were a Fourth of July fireworks. No way in the world was I going to let this lecherous man think that my experience had given him an invitation to start a relationship with me. I wanted him out of my face. I was paying him by the hour to work on my computer, and he had been working for several hours prior to my almost accident, and there he was still in my home. Either he was milking the hours or was incompetent. No matter—I wanted no part of him.

I do feel blessed and watched over. I've heard stories from other pet sitters about close calls they've had with people setting up appointments in their home to meet their animal and then something didn't seem right about the person, location, or something else. A married woman told me about calling on her husband for backup when she went to visit a potential client, and indeed, the client had a criminal background. This pet sitter had listened to her intuition, her gut, her feeling that something wasn't right. Thank heaven she paid attention to her promptings from above.

I have felt for a long time that we all have a power pack, yes, like Cesar Milan's description of his dogs as a power pack. The power pack I believe in follows each one of us; it consists of all our loved ones who have gone to heaven and are watching over us. I think our parents, grandparents, great-grandparents, aunts, uncles, brothers, sisters, friends, cats, dogs, horses, hamsters, and others whom we loved and still love are indeed our power pack. Of course, I am sure that we also have many angels looking over us.

I have walked dogs at ten, eleven, and even twelve at night many times; it's a great time to walk. Our summer days in Florida can have temperatures over 100 degrees. Most homes have AC, so animals and people get used to an environment ranging from seventy to eighty degrees inside. Because dogs don't sweat, walking in the heat of the day can overheat and kill them. I've watched a dog die from heat stroke, and it wasn't pleasant.

No, his death had nothing to do with me. I was in the animal emergency with an ill kitten when a family walked in carrying their dog, which was suffering from being kept outside in the hot sun for far too long. My heart was broken when I saw him and then again when I looked at the five-year-old girl who was devastated by his death. That need not have happened. I prefer walking dogs at night because it's cooler and we both enjoy the walk. Most people have gone to bed by then, so we rarely encounter anyone on our walks. I like being able to arrive later in the morning. I tend to be a night owl, so that works well for me. In fact this very moment it is 4:15 AM as I am editing my writing.

I have also found that most people are afraid of all big dogs, but very few big dogs need to be feared. I've walked Labrador Retrievers, Weimaraners, Golden Retrievers, and other big dogs that seemed to scare passers-by. These breeds in particular are total sweethearts and love muffins. But people's lack of knowledge is good for me because they give me a wide berth when they pass me on the sidewalk. They might even cross to the other side of the road, and that's fine with me. I feel like Moses parting the Red Sea when I walk my pittie, Abbott. He is a brindle sweetheart; however, people tinkle in their frillies when they see him and cross the street. I'm glad they do. I don't want any scared witless person doing something stupid.

I have always felt protected. I cannot explain why or how I feel protected, but I do. I firmly believe that my power pack is always with me. A few times, I may have felt that somewhere or somehow, something wasn't right when I have been walking a dog in a dark neighborhood. When that has happened, I think, *Dear God and all the angels, please protect me.* They've always come to my aid because I have never had any problems. Thank you, God.

Nine out of ten times when I talk to God, I thank him rather than ask him for something. My prayer has been the following.

> Dear God,
>
> Thank you for this wonderful business and the wonderful people you have brought into my life through it. Thank you for my excellent health so that I can handle this business. And thank for the excellent health of all my children.

Yep … that's it—simple, honest, and to the point. The attitude of gratitude is the best attitude to have.

The phrase "all my children" includes all the animals on this planet. Yes, when I become a family's pet sitter, I become the grandmother of that pet.

After the tragedy of 9/11, I heard and saw so many people devastated, debilitated, and panicked by fear. I took some time out and asked myself how I felt about 9/11. After some consideration, I decided not to live in fear, which accomplishes nothing. Fear is paralyzing. If you fear the enemy, the enemy has won the battle.

I don't go to church. I work seven days a week. I also have no church clothes. All my clothes are for dog walking and other animal care, and all my clothes are stained and spotted even after repeated washings. However, I watch Joel Osteen on my computer and television, and I always have him talking to me in my car. My pets have spent countless hours listening to Joel, who like St. Francis, preaches to the animals whether or not he is aware of that. I have told many people that I walk with JC and JO.

Chapter 19

Vehicle Breakdowns

One of the great pluses of being a pet sitter is that I can run home between visits to other homes and see my children. I can feed them, let them out to tinkle and play, and possibly even have lunch or dinner myself. That's a plus. Also, when the weather is mild, I can take a best friend with me.

I used to take Her Royal Highness Amelia Elizabeth with me. She was and still is my heart, my soul, my nose, my toes—the best half of me. She would ride along with me each day and patiently sit in the car. I would then go into a home and come outside walking with a dog or dogs from that home. Afterward, I would walk Amy for a short walk in that same neighborhood. Then we would drive to another home and do the same thing again. She was my copilot, my best friend, and I still miss her with all my soul.

One evening, Amy and I were driving well after sunset. In front of us, a large semitrailer truck pulled out of a shopping center parking lot onto the major six-lane highway into the southbound lane I was in. As it pulled onto the highway, I noted that it had precious few reflectors or lights on the sides of the trailer. It seemed as though I were looking at a large, grey, empty movie screen. I slowed down. A car came up behind me and passed on my left. The driver obviously hadn't seen the trailer clearly. I was not at all surprised to see the car veer to the right as it tried to avoid hitting the semi. When it hit the semi, parts of the car flew all over the road. I slowed down more and tried to avoid the debris. I ran over something that gave me a flat. I limped to a Dunkin'

Donuts and called a tow truck. The tow truck came, and I showed him my AAA card.

When Amy and I started to climb into his cab, the driver told me that Amy couldn't ride in his cab. He said she could ride in my jeep, which was strapped onto the back of his tow truck. I said that if she had to ride back there, I would as well. He said I couldn't do that. I was livid! I said that if she rode in the jeep and it went flying off the truck and crashed and killed her, that would be all right, but if I were in the jeep too and it crashed and killed me, that would not be all right!

Of course he said I was correct. Damn. I was mad! I yelled, "We'll figure this out!"

I told him to leave with my jeep; Amy and I would take a cab home, which we did. I was infuriated. I've had to call multiple tow trucks over the years, and many of the drivers have had their dogs with them. I was just unlucky enough to get a spaghetti-for-brains, anal-retentive, woman-and-animal hater that night.

Chapter 20

Border Collie Time

Border collie time is any time I am awake caring for my fur children. If that takes me from early in the morning to late in the evening, so be it. There isn't anything I won't do for an animal no matter how time consuming it may be; I care for the animal the best I can. That's what I'm paid to do, but I don't do it for the pay. I do it to care for the health, safety, and security of the home and animals. I watch over the home and animals there just as a border collie watches over a flock of defenseless sheep that depend on the dog.

I provide whatever an animal needs or wants. I know when they are happy, sad, fearful, and playful; I am there for them, not for the pay. One might snicker and say, "Yeah, sure." Well, after twenty-six years of loving my sweethearts, I will share with you one item.

I go above and beyond what is expected of me in a client's home for only one reason—for the animals. When I arrive, I greet them, love them, and take care of food, water, medications, and anything else involved. Then it's our time to interact.

I mention this because I feel like a border collie—always moving for a purpose. My hugging, kissing, petting, and praising each fur baby have a purpose. I want them all to know I adore them.

I realize how many commitments families have mired their lives into nothingness with. It seems to be a nationwide affliction. Fluffy is usually only patted on the head and then left home alone while the family members go to the fitness center, yoga class, dancing class, shopping, taking the car in for an oil change, on and on. They love

Fluffy for five seconds at a time. They let Fluffy out to pee or to do his business, but once Fluffy's back inside, it's back to business as usual. That means they have no time to notice maybe a small growth on Fluffy's body. Maybe they throw dry food into a bowl once daily and don't even notice if all of it is eaten or possibly even regurgitated later because there was something nasty in the food. Many times, they buy the cheapest pet food because they consider grooming and vet bills are too high as it is.

I've encountered families with huge homes, several cars, and significant incomes who have purchased a purebred Fluffy for several thousand dollars. Then all I hear from them is how expensive the vet is, how expensive the groomer is, how expensive the dog food is, and sometimes how expensive my services may be. All the while, this family of five is going to go away for a week or two to Europe or the Caribbean and more than once a year.

I've walked into homes and noticed that the water bowl had pink scum all over the inside of the dish. No one had cared to toss out "old water" and then at least wipe out the dish with a paper towel before refilling with fresh water. I've washed brown bowls that dry kibble had been tossed into daily and seen them turn from brown to white, blue, green—whatever color the bowl actually was—because the dog's saliva and food crumbs had adhered to the unwashed bowl. I'm not germ phobic, but I wouldn't want to analyze what bacteria might be alive and well in such water and food bowls. I have no problem washing these dishes and presenting fresh water and fresh kibble to Fluffy. I wash my hands with regular soap but never use a hand sanitizer, and I'm the healthiest person in this county.

Such families don't love their pets. When each family member is sitting with ears and eyes glued to their cell phones or computers, Fluffy might as well be on another planet. People, put your eyes and heart in Fluffy's place. Just do it!

The most important part of each visit I make to my clients' pets is the time I spend with them playing and talking. Particularly if the family has little time for Fluffy, I want him to know I love and cherish him. I am Abby in *The Help*; I tell each fur baby, "You is kind, you is smart, and you is important." I want to ensure that when I meet all the fur babies in heaven, I will be welcomed without reservation. If only animals were at heaven's gate, I would be happier than I have ever been!

Chapter 21

Karma Indeed Works

I have seen it time and time again, but never have I seen it work in twenty-four hours until this one particular situation.

I had a client who had a sweet little Lhasa Apso. This client had me watch her for a few days when she went out of town. After she returned, we remained in touch with one another.

One day, she called to tell me that her dog hadn't been eating; her groomer had told her that her dog would die if it didn't eat. I told her that her baby needed to see a vet right away. I recommended Blue Pearl Veterinary, and I was very happy I did.

The assessment by Blue Pearl was pyometria, a major inflammation of the uterus that occurs spontaneously and is fatal if not addressed immediately. This sweet dear needed a total abdominal hysterectomy, in medical terms, a bilingualsalpingoophorectomy. Everything associated with reproduction had to be removed. I know because I had had that procedure.

When the vet made the diagnosis, the woman remarked that the dog actually belonged to her daughter, who lived in California. We called her from the vet's office and explained the situation. The surgery was going to be expensive, and the vet needed to be assured of payment.

The daughter said she didn't have the money, so Care Credit was suggested. She had to go online and see if she qualified for Care Credit. She did indeed qualify, so plans were put in place to immediately perform surgery on this sweetheart.

We left the vet's office, and I needed to see pups at a home. I asked the woman if she minded riding along with me. She didn't drive, and I didn't want to slip my schedule any further by taking her home first.

We got to my client's home, and I let the dogs out into the fenced backyard for some play and tinkle time. I went to my car to check on the woman. She told me that she had just received a phone call from the veterinarian's office. The office told her that they had just received a call from her daughter to stop the surgery. They explained that the surgery had already started and couldn't be stopped. Her daughter's change of mind puzzled us.

On the way home, I asked her why her dear little girl dog had not been spayed when she was a puppy. I listened and was dumbfounded with the explanation. She said that when they had first acquired the dog, they had plans to show her. However, they ended up not putting her in the show ring because of a dog handler's assessment. They were told that her teeth needed straightening and that would require braces. At that time, this woman and her husband had a boy and girl, so the expense of braces for the dog was out of the question.

In time, the children grew up and the daughter moved to California. Prior to the surgery, this woman had bragged about her daughter having a great job in California. She told of her daughter having Fendi purses that cost $5,000. Well, God bless her. I have never seen one and cannot imagine anyone paying $5,000 for any purse. She explained that her daughter's entire apartment was white and that the dog would make it dirty and that the daughter couldn't have the dog with her because she worked such long hours.

Okay … whatever the story is, it is.

The next day, I drove to this woman's home to take her to Blue Pearl to see her sweet dear. During the drive, she said that she had talked with her daughter earlier in the day. The daughter had told her that her boyfriend had just ended their relationship and that her daughter had been so upset that she went out for the evening with her girlfriend; they had several drinks, and on the way home, she was stopped for speeding and charged with driving under the influence. She told her mother she had to pay $5,000 to bail herself out of jail.

Okay, you can connect the dots as well as I can. Twenty-four-hour karma.

Chapter 22

Christmas 2008, Pet Sitting

Everything that can go wrong will go wrong at the most inopportune time.

Christmas pet sitting is the busiest time of year for all pet sitters. However, this is when the most time-consuming and extraordinary events seem to occur. In 2008, I encountered the following.

The night before the pet sitting started, I got a call from a neighbor. A cat lover in the neighborhood had discovered that a six-week-old, partially feral kitten had a broken lower jaw. He didn't know whom else to call. Pet sitters can be called for a thousand different emergencies real and imagined. This happens because the person has no idea who else to call during their emergency of the moment.

I made some phone calls and found out that one of our emergency facilities works with the SPCA in situations such as that. The gentleman and I gathered up this dear kitten, and I drove to the emergency facility. I spent $100 to have the kitten's injuries assessed. The kitten was in perfect health except for its broken lower jaw. The prognosis wasn't good. I learned that both canine teeth were missing—not a good thing. The vet explained that in such cases, the lower jaw was wired to stabilize it, and the canine teeth were crucial for this procedure. We signed the kitten over to the facility and said our prayers.

On the way home, the gentleman and I saw an entire neighborhood decorated for Christmas. All kinds of cars were driving through. A sign stated that a certain radio station was broadcasting the Christmas music that the displays were synchronized with. It was also a fundraiser for a children's charity. We contributed to the charity as we drove through and enjoyed the display.

No folks, I didn't do that because I had gotten the kitten issue placed in another person's lap! The kind gentleman and I were brokenhearted after leaving the emergency vet's office. I felt in some way that this Christmas cheer was a healing balm for our broken hearts.

I learned that this man fed feral cats and kittens in our condo complex. He told me that he wanted me to meet a woman who had loved a German shepherd that had passed on. He said that she had loved this shepherd so much that when the dog lost a tooth, the woman had it replaced with a gold tooth. I wanted to meet her and get her story, but I wasn't able to.

The next morning, I was feeding my kitties and dressing to start my day when I noticed my kitties looking outside my screen porch. I walked over, looked down, and saw a pigeon. I wondered what the significance of that pigeon was. I looked up "pigeon" in Ted Andrews's animal totem book, and one of the four explanations seemed to apply more than any other. It stated that when a pigeon appears, it signifies that a soul just recently made its transition from its earthly body into spirit. I knew in my heart that Charlie, the six-week-old partially feral kitten with the broken jaw had been euthanized. Such moments are poignant.

The busiest time of year began with two of my families leaving on the same day, so I had to visit one home three times daily for two weeks to let their three puppies out of their crates to run, play, eat, drink, tinkle, and poo. I visited the other home twice daily to feed their kitty and care for their bird. This kitty was an old friend of mine, and I knew her very well.

However, even the most seasoned pet sitter forgets the limits set by her precious wonderfuls. I petted and loved Janie, and she loved every minute of my attention. Then all of a sudden she attacked my hand. Yikes! Pain ... blood. Not just blood—it was like Old Faithful in Yellowstone Park. Yes, one tooth had punctured a vein. I picked up her food dish and carried it into the house because I needed something to catch the geyser of blood before it hit the floor.

Just the beginning of the Christmas pet-sitting season and there I was getting bitten. Horrors of all horrors if this turned into a media event in the ER. I told myself, *No, not this time! This one will heal on its own and won't force me to make a visit to the ER.* I went to the kitchen sink and ran cold water over my wrist to help clot the blood and stop the bleeding. I went to the bathroom and rummaged around for bandages, which I found along with a bottle of hydrogen peroxide. I poured a gallon of it over my arm to make sure that all puncture wounds and been sanitized. After covering several inches of my wrist with the lovely bandages, I told Janie and Max that I would be back in the morning.

By the way, Janie was not rabid, mean, or anything else ... she was just Janie. She was an indoor kitty who was totally adored and cared for extremely well. I had obviously crossed some invisible line, and she reminded me that she didn't approve of my actions.

I didn't have three days to spend in a hospital as I had previously due to a cat bite; it was just the beginning of the Christmas pet-sitting season, and I needed to make visits to eight homes daily and care for my own children. I dosed myself mightily with vitamin C and Microhydrin tablets over the next several days. Eventually, I realized that my arm was not red or swelling and didn't have any red streaks *Woo hoo!* I had avoided the hospital.

Then another family left town; I had arranged to stay overnight at their home. Their beagle was ill, and we were hoping I could keep this dear one alive until they came back. The sweetheart had been in kidney failure for months. She was at the point that she had been refusing the food provided by the vet for kidney failure.

The family had consulted with me about putting her down before they left town. I told them to feed her anything she would eat. There comes a time when the quality of life means more than the quantity of life. I stayed with this dear baby for several days and nights; finally, she said goodbye and went over the Rainbow Bridge. I felt so sorry for the family as I had known them and their sweet beagle for many years. These people were the greatest people you would ever want to meet. I know how much they grieved when their dear Snoopy went to heaven.

Well, so much for celebrating the holidays at least for this pet sitter. I was emotionally and physically exhausted and ready for some downtime.

I had taken care of Snoopy many times over the years, and she had even gone with me to schools when I visited once per year. Yes, I visited schoolchildren to explain what a pet sitter did for animals whenever a family went out of town. Snoopy was always adored by them. Really now, who doesn't love Snoopy?

Chapter 23

Thank You Means So Much to a Pet Sitter

The following letter was a lovely gift to me. It means so much to people when they get a written thank you note or full letter as this woman sent me.

Hi Fran:

I don't know if you're going to remember me, but we met a couple of months ago at Florida Veterinary Specialists. As I was paying for some food, we struck up a conversation. I told you about my male cat, Brewser, who has IBS (irritable bowel syndrome), and what a hard time I had been having getting his condition under control.

After spending over a $1,000 at Florida Veterinary Specialists and many visits to my personal vet, nothing has worked completely. That had been going on for almost two years and was very frustrating.

During our conversation, you recommended that I try raw meat purchased from Your Natural Pet in Dunedin.

I visited the store that following Saturday and spoke to Julie (what a sweet person she is), and she helped me select what she thought would be appealing to my cat.

I've experimented with several of the varieties and have settled on the Oman raw rabbit. Brewser loves it! I mix some raw vegetables with it that I puree in my blender and add a scoop of the Nupro Nuggets vitamins. I'm happy to say he is 100 percent better. The best part is that I have been able to cut back on his medication to about a quarter of the amount. I am hopeful I can get him off the prednisone completely.

I haven't talked to my vet yet to let him know what I'm doing. I wanted to wait until I'm sure this is a cure.

I just wanted to let you know how thankful I am for your advice. It's amazing, after spending so much time and money with the "experts," that you seem to be so much more in tune to what needed to be done. Thank you!

I stopped at the store on Saturday, and Julie said I had just missed you by about five minutes. I tried to call you on your cell but didn't leave a message, so I just wanted to drop you an email mainly to let you know how much I appreciated your help … and so does Brewser. He's a much happier feline these days :>).

Hope you have a wonderful holiday, and if I ever need your pet-sitting services, I will give you a call. I'm passing the word to my friends as well.

Shar Kraycik

I always try to help people with any of their needs concerning their babies. Over the years, I have studied diet and nutrition for myself and my animals. I try to offer advice whenever it is needed if I feel I might have a solution. I always try to cure any ailment in a simplistic and usually organic fashion before relenting and recommending a visit to a veterinarian. Those visits always seem to result in the administration of poisons from big pharma.

I feel sorry for most vets, who are funded and trained by big pharma. The worst part is that they don't think outside the box. I'm always learning and gathering information from multiple sources to make informed decisions. I value holistic and simplistic treatment of all ailments whenever possible. I have worked with Reiki masters when my Amy was being treated for her cancer. I have tried laser therapy and Cell Quest liquid, which is made from plantains. I didn't just believe every word uttered by the oncologist we were working with. By the way, ten-plus years later, I still love and adore Dr. Kane, who did everything possible to eradicate cancer in my heart and soul, HRH Amelia Elizabeth. He is a very special angel.

I wish we all took our health and the health of our loved ones into their own hands and not rely completely on any one person for a cure. Over time, I've developed the ability to look at an animal and know that he or she is ill or in distress. I once looked into the face of a stranger and knew he had Alzheimer's. When that happened, his wife asked me how I knew. I told her that I didn't know how I knew; I'd just sensed it when I observed him for a minute or two. Maybe I read energy as animals read energy. I don't know.

Shar's sweet letter made me feel like a million dollars. I was so happy to have been able to help her baby. Drugs can kill, and long-term use of any drug can be life altering for the animal.

Besides giving advice, pet sitters rescue animals. The letter below describes a pet- sitter friend of mine in Tampa. I am so proud of her. She witnessed a man dumping two wee kittens in a residential neighborhood, and she didn't hesitate for a second to spring into action and rescue those kittens. She's made of the right stuff. God bless you, Missy.

These two emails were sent to me by one of my lifelong clients after I had sent her my letter describing Missy's kitty rescue. My client and her husband are fantastic kitty parents, and I wanted her to read this true story. We need great stories to help us remember that there are great and totally decent people on this planet who have great characters and spring into action in an instant to do the right thing.

Hi Fran,

God bless this woman! I loved this email … actually, I wanted to sic the Police out after this fool that dumped the babies! Someone needs to dump him or his loved ones in the trash!

Thank goodness this woman was there in the right place, and right time. I would love to know that these babies got adopted. I am sure that others would also love to hear when these babies get adopted! Thanks so much for this! We will speak with you soon! Monet, Mia, and Paris send their "MEOWS" and they said that they can't wait until you come and take care of them in January!

All of my best, Rachel

I recently purchased the book *Behaving as if the God in All Life Mattered*. The story below is about a young woman who behaves as if the God in all life did matter.

I heard an incredible story this evening. A pet-sitter friend of mine in Tampa saw a man in an SUV with a cardboard box. He was stopped in a residential neighborhood. She slowed down to clearly observe him. It appeared that he had two kittens that he was trying to round up. Wrong! He hopped back into his vehicle and sped away after dumping the cats.

My friend was horrified. She stopped and rounded the two up. She has multiple animals at her home, including two FIV-positive cats she doesn't want to expose another cat to. She called a woman in Tampa who rescued ferals and other unwanted kitties. She tried to find a foster home for these two. No luck.

She went to Florida Veterinary Services to try to beg someone to take them. They had twenty-one cats there, and everyone had several at home. She was totally distraught as she could only think of taking these two babies to animal control. She knew that would mean certain death.

She called the woman who fostered the feral kitties and found them homes one more time. While she was on the phone with her, she got a call from a foster home; it could take the kittens in two weeks.

My friend went back to Florida Veterinary Services and said, "*Pleeeeze*, can anyone foster these babies for just two weeks?" Someone said that a new vet in Brandon might. They called this vet, who said yes.

My friend drove these two babies to Brandon from North Tampa; she said that she would have driven to Tallahassee if need be.

While driving, she related this story to me and told me how the two babies were snuggling and grooming each other. She hoped that they could be adopted together.

While she was at Florida Veterinary Services, the babies were tested for Feline Leukemia and AIDS, and both were negative … Whoopee! They had some fleas and had received medication for that. So as I bed down for the night and as my friend Missy beds down for the night, we are happy and at peace.

Thank you very much, God, for all the people who care enough to actually become involved and make a difference in the wee ones' lives.

By the way, when Missy saw this man dumping the kitties, she was on her way to pick up her mother. It was her mother's birthday, and they were going to do something special together. As you can well imagine, their special plans were pushed into the next day. I know Missy's mother had no problem with the change of plans.

Chapter 24

Pure Joy ... This Is a Happy Life Now!

Okay, I'm blubbering again. I just watched a wonderful movie that starred a Border Collie. I was tearing up and welling up with incredible love while watching this dog rescue several children from a forest fire. Oh my, did that get to me!

It got to me because I have always known the heart of a dog. Ever since I was a child growing up on a farm, I've loved everything about every animal. I played outside all day with my best friend, Pat. Pat was a solid black long haired dog who had been rescued from the streets of Indianapolis by my uncle. She had been at my great grandmother's home and then she came to our home. Everyone in the family knew how much I adored her. We spent many hours walking in the woods. Yes, a young girl and her best friend. Human friends were not there for me. I was thought of as "dumb" or "retarded" because I stuttered. I also loved and played with my grandfather's foxhounds and his beagle named Timmy.

Here I am, nearly seventy-three, and I remember each sweetheart distinctly in my heart and mind. Love never dies, and the feelings you register while you're giving and receiving love never die.

I have the most incredible respect for the godlike goodness of animals and their awesome intelligence. I have always felt it, known it, and needed it throughout my life. I have always had animals in my life. They are my safe place. They always heal me. I in turn know without a doubt that every animal in my life knows that he or she *is* my life.

I do not trust people. People are fickle—that's one of the nicest comments I can make about people. Human animals contribute negative energy to their surroundings while all other animals contribute love to their environments. After all, all there is is love. The Beatles sang that over fifty years ago, and it's true today.

My first soul-to-soul encounter with an animal happened nearly thirty years ago at a renaissance fair, where knights in shining armor rode great steeds and jousted while maidens bedecked in period costumes passed out bouquets of wildflowers—idyllic.

At one point, I was standing near a pony ride for children. You've seen them many times—ponies in a circle giving children rides. I was just a few feet away from a pony when our eyes met. I was overwhelmed with the most intense sadness and despair. I had no idea what I could have done to ease the poor pony's pain. I felt that his spirit had been crushed a long time ago and he was reaching out to me for help. I had to walk away and leave that dear soul to endure his agony. Here I am years later wishing I could have done something for him.

Animals notice something different about me. Time and again, I've had dogs I didn't know being walked on sidewalks start to pull toward me while I was in my car sitting still at a red light. I wish I could talk to the animals and find out what precipitates such behavior. I've taken classes and read books on animal communication because I've always wanted to talk with them very badly.

Then Whoopie came to live with me and my pack. She is a very happy party girl. I have no idea how she got the name Whoopie, but it fits her well. My Sunshine—oops, I mean Whoopie—has told me that this is a happy life now. Yes she did.

Over twelve years ago, I took in a rescue dog named Sunshine. She was approximately ten, and she was among three hundred plus dogs rescued by animal groups in Florida from a compound of over 600 dogs in Opp, Alabama. Texas and Illinois stepped in to save several hundred dogs. Sunshine was the second dog I took in from that horrid compound.

When she came to me, she had multiple eye, ear, and urinary tract infections. Her nails were three inches long. Her hearing was nearly gone, and her abuse had led her to distrust anyone of my size and shape. I found out quickly that whenever I was wearing a dark, solid-color T-shirt and blue jeans, I looked to her like her previous abusers. I quickly learned that if I wore nothing or a dress or any clothing that was light colored, I was not a threat to her. I discovered that whenever I would pick up the TV remote control, she would come snarling at me, growling with teeth bared because her poor eyesight told her that I was holding a stick and I was going to strike her. Poor dear.

Once I realized all the triggers, I was prepared to deal with the aggression. After all, she had nowhere to go. Not one person in the county wanted her, and the humane society that had rescued her would do nothing but put her down because of her fear and aggression. Lawsuits do happen, and they always did their best to avoid being sued. So there I was, the bad guy who was her caretaker. We had to work this out.

Whenever she growled at me, I'd stand still with both hands behind my back—no flailing of hands and arms. Sunshine had endured enough flailing hands, arms, and objects. I would look her in the eyes and would say repeatedly in a very calm, slow voice, "Sunshine, go lie down," until Sunshine would walk away from me. I repeated it twenty, thirty, forty times—whatever it took to get her to walk away. I had to win the confrontation each time because she had no home to live in but mine. Sunshine had had most of her teeth broken off because of the prior beatings with sticks, so eating hard kibble was not easy for her.

Around that same time I had acquired a wonderful new friend, Barbara Fiala, a lifelong canine behaviorist and dog trainer. When I told her of Sunshine's lack of teeth, Barbara suggested that I mix boiled macaroni and wet dog food, and that worked well.

Sunshine never wanted to go outside. I would imagine that having been in a ten-by-ten enclosure exposed to the wind, rain, snow, and hot sun for several years had made her appreciate being inside. Also, because of her prior abuse and fears, she would not allow a leash to be attached to her collar so that she could be walked outside. I would get her outside at feeding time by carrying her bowl to a slab of concrete in the backyard and walk away. I then would go back into my home leaving the back door open. She would go out and eat, wander out into our securely fenced backyard, and tinkle and poo. When she was finished, I let her back in. Day after day, I worked with her fears, which were hard to overcome.

The best we can do is fill each baby's mind with wonderful, loving actions daily so painful memories can be pushed back further and further in their memory banks. I wanted her to not react out of fear; I thought it pitiful that she would live in fear of anything.

Maybe a year or two later, Sunshine was much more at home with me. She realized she was safe and not subject to abuse any more. At that time when I knew that she felt safe in our home I noticed that her entire face looked younger. Yes, it truly did look younger and happier!

One day, she became ill, and we were told that it was probably her heart; she went to heaven. I was always so glad that before she went to heaven, she had been loved. I couldn't bear to think of her being treated so badly and possibly going to heaven without ever knowing a loving human or a safe home.

After she went to heaven, I left my abusive husband and lived in a condo. We had never divorced, so twelve years later, when he died, I got my home back because it had been in both of our names. It was wonderful to be back; I could start the next chapter of my life.

About then, a dog rescue asked me if I could take in a dog, and I of course said yes. Here came Whoopie, whom I had mentioned earlier. Her family had lost their home and had to give her up. As I said, her name fits her personality perfectly. She is the happiest, most playful sweetheart this old soul had seen in a long time.

After she had been with me for about six months, the most incredible thing occurred. I was in my favorite chair and had my feet stretched out in front of me on my footstool. The next thing I knew, Whoopie was wedged between my chair and footstool demanding attention—she wanted to play. I was calling her Whoopie Doodles and laughing, and all of a sudden the name Sunshine came out of my mouth! I was astounded … Why had that happened? No one was in the room, I hadn't been thinking about Sunshine, but her name just popped out of my mouth. Almost instantly, I understood that Whoopie *was* Sunshine—an epiphany! I put my hands on her back and said, "Oh my God! You're Sunshine!" I wanted her to know that I knew it was her.

I heard in my heart, *I was Sunshine. I'm Whoopie now. This is a happy life now.* I heard a voice in my ear as if a telephone line was connecting my ear to my heart. I can't explain what I said in the last sentence, but I sensed she and I had a heart-to-heart connection. Oh heavens to Betsy! You could have knocked me over with a feather. But I understood—she wanted no reminders of her old life as Sunshine. She was living a happy life, and her name, Whoopie, even more so made that fact very pronounced to both of us.

That event was the most important game changer in my life. Over the years, I had lost a great many babies. I was always left so bereft and crushed by each loss. It took me many months and sometimes years to fully get over the loss of my best friend. I felt I was walking around bumping into walls. I didn't feel human for many months due to my grief.

When Whoopie told me who she was, I was elated. I knew that love never dies and that our loved ones never leave us.

My gosh, why couldn't I have learned that many years ago? The pain and suffering I endured each time I lost a loved one was debilitating, and getting over the loss of a loved one was always a painfully slow process. I think of all the time I spent being sad when I could have been joyful and thus healthier and happier. That period of pain and sadness did not need to occur. My loved one was whole, happy, and at peace all the while and more than likely standing beside me trying to bring me peace, closure, and happiness so I would no longer suffer.

None of our loved ones want us to be sad and walking around like dead people after we've lost them. Why on earth would they want us to suffer if they loved and adored us as much as we loved and adored them? I wondered why the universe hadn't allowed me to discover this wonderful truth many years ago so I wouldn't have agonized over the loss of one of my loved ones for weeks, months, or even years. What was the point of waiting until I attained the incredibly young age of sixty-seven before the universe allowed me to discover this truth? What did my waiting until now accomplish?

Many people give up on love when they have been hurt with such loss. Then of course they wither and die. How in the world would their pain, suffering, and death due to intense grief serve any purpose in this universe?

In my many years of pet sitting, I have heard people say, "When my dog dies, I'm not getting another one because I can't stand the pain of losing another sweetheart." I feel it's my God-given mission to let them know that love never dies and that their babies will return to them. If they think they can't take the pain of loss even one more time and they close the door to love, they are shutting out their sweethearts. But if they keep an open heart, their sweethearts will return to them in their own time and perhaps in a circuitous fashion. If they walk all over searching for their sweethearts, they will never find them. The universe will return their dear ones to them in its own way and time, not ours.

What a bitch, huh? You're decimated and want your baby back instantly, but that's not going to happen. Whoopie came back to me when I was settled back into the home I loved (sans husband), and then she and I could both have happy lives.

Trust in the universe. It knows what it's doing, and it's all for our highest and best good.

Chapter 25

Always Trust Your Intuition, Your Gut, and Your Feelings

One time, I had a hunch about something. I paid attention, and thank God I did. I had been staying at a home for two weeks while the husband and wife were away. They had two kitties and two puppies. This family allowed their kitties to be indoor and outdoor kitties. I had taken care of them multiple times, and nothing had happened to them.

After nearly a week there, I was putting one kitty on the table to eat his food and felt something wet on his chest. I examined it and thought he needed a vet. I got an appointment for that afternoon. The vet discovered he had an abscess. Since he was an indoor and outdoor kitty, we guessed he had been in a cat fight; abscesses due to cat fights are all too common.

The vet sedated Halo, cleaned the wound, and gave him an antibiotic that would last about two weeks, so no daily pills would be needed. The vet installed a drain and placed a bandage over the wound and drain. She slipped a light weight netting that was like a stretchy T-shirt on his chest to hold the drain and bandage in place and keep him from licking the spot.

I was told to keep Halo in the house in a quiet room for seven to ten days. Since this kitty was used to always being outside at will, I had no idea if I would have a howling angry Halo or a calm Halo to deal with.

We got home, and I shut him in the living room with food, water, and a litter box. The two dogs and I could stay in the family room that had access to another room. The other room had a large doggie door as well as a sliding door.

Halo did very well the first night and day in the room, so I thought that if I shut the doggie door, Halo could join me and the two dogs in the family room. After several hours of not seeing or hearing Halo, I started feeling uneasy. Cats sleep a lot, and Halo was quiet, but something didn't feel right. I searched the house but couldn't find him. I instantly went to check on the doggie door and saw that it had been raised about three inches. *Aww shit!* It was dark then. I knew Halo had to be outside. I told myself to stay calm as I opened the sliding door and stepped out onto the deck.

I was peering into the darkness and calmly calling out, "Halo, Halo." Unbelievably, I saw him lying on the ground about five feet in front of me gazing up at me. He was very, very calm. Thank you, Lord! I got a grip on myself and walked toward him as calmly as I could. Animals can sense stress and tense musculature, and the last thing I wanted was for him to bolt into the dark. I talked sweetly and softly to him. Thank God he stayed put on the ground. I gently lifted him and cuddled him like a child. Of course while doing that, I nearly fell over twice because I was wearing nothing but stockings on my feet and I was stepping in small foxholes the two dogs had dug all over the yard.

I begged God not to let me fall and drop this kitty. I don't know how in the world I didn't fall down, but I carried this sweetheart into the home and back into the original room in which he had been sequestered. Oh Lord, thanks for letting Halo be relaxed and lying just a few feet away from me. Thank heaven there was just enough light emanating from the inside of the home for me to see him lying there in the grass. I thanked God and all the angels over and over once Halo was safe in his room and my heart started beating once more.

With that elastic knit shirt encompassing him from his head to his abdomen, I could just imagine him anywhere at all out in the yard or neighborhood. He could be tangled up in a bush or fighting another cat or meeting a coyote.

All I can say is, trust your gut always!

Chapter 26

Never Interrupt a Jaguar's Hunt

Blackie and the Rat

I have had many overnights at several homes over the years. I always have all kinds of experiences at each home, but this one was unique. One home had several dogs and two cats. The property was fenced, and the home had a doggie door.

One evening, I was in the bedroom watching TV with Molly, a Basset Hound, and we were eating. I was spending all the time I could with her because she had recently been diagnosed with bladder cancer. She had an amazing personality, and I adored her. I even nicknamed her: The Divine Miss M!! She was absolutely adorable and no one could ever deny her anything she wanted!!!!

I walked to the kitchen to return a plate that had contained some watermelon juice and seeds; I was being careful not to drip any of the juice. In the kitchen was Blackie, who was incredibly black, strong, and capable. I noticed he was poised, just waiting for the appropriate moment to attack. Attack what? I knew that he was fixated on something. However, the plate I was holding gingerly was blocking my view of the floor. I stood still and thought about what Blackie was fixated on and to my surprise something bit my big toe! Yikes, did that hurt!

I realized Blackie had chased a rat into the home via the doggie door and had cornered the rat in the kitchen. Lucky me—I wandered in at just the right time to break up this standoff between the two. I yelped in surprise and pain, and off the rat skittered. Only God knew where and believe me when I say, "I did not care!"

I put the plate down on the counter and said, "Blackie, I'll let you take care of this." I made an about-face and walked back to Molly.

The two-story home had several bedrooms and nooks and crannies; there were eight million places where a small animal could hide, so there was no point in my pursuing the rat. Besides, Blackie was doing an extremely good job of trailing it.

I went to the bedroom and slept with Molly and several other wonderful babies who lived in this home. Business as usual …

The next day, someone I bumped into remarked, "That rat could have had rabies." I had never thought about that. I thought I'd stop in at the humane society, where I knew most of the employees, and ask them about rabies. Wouldn't you know? No one there knew the answer. At the humane society no less!

I got them wondering; however, and one of them got the idea to call the Clearwater Parks Department. They inquired about rats having rabies and were told, "Rodents don't get rabies." Thank heaven!

Later, when I told Blackie's parents about my experience, I related another incident. At another home, I was caring for two dogs that started fighting each other. Supposedly, they got along just fine—roommates in the same home, no problems. However, maybe they were fighting over Nanny Fran's attention and got irritated at one another. Maybe jealousy entered the picture?

I couldn't even walk them together without their fighting one another. Two beagles! I couldn't believe that was happening. I separated them and called their family to tell them about the problem. Of course they were incredulous, and I was too.

When the Jaguar's family returned, I told them about their rat visitor and the two quarreling beagles. The husband said, "If it weren't for bad luck, you'd have no luck at all." Some days are like that.

Chapter 27

Fingerprints, Fingerprints

One story related to me was screamingly funny! A pet sitter had been notified by a client that a home across the street from her home had animals in it. The neighbor was concerned because one person had moved out because of nonpayment of rent. Another person was still there but was having several people coming and going at odd hours and doors were left open. She thought that the young man there was dealing drugs. The woman had observed a cat in the living room window from time to time, and she didn't consider the place a safe environment for any animal. Somehow, this woman knew that the person living there was moving and was not planning on taking the cat.

Jane, as I will call the woman, and Karen, as I will call the pet sitter, were worried that the cat might meet an untimely demise. Jane went to the home in the daytime and slipped inside through an open door in the rear of the home. She saw a ripped-open bag of dog food on the kitchen floor. She walked through the house and found the kitty in the back bedroom. He was sitting behind a mattress and box spring that were leaning up against the wall. She had dishes with her for water and food, and she placed them behind the mattress and box spring with the kitty. She said she saw no other food or water dishes for the kitty, but she did spot a litter box that was overflowing with kitty poo.

Jane remarked that all at once it dawned on her that it was ten in the morning. The renter could have walked in at any time; she was trespassing. She then left the home as quickly as possible and told Karen what she had found.

That night, they returned with flashlights and a cat carrier. Jane led the way into the house with flashlights pointed to the floor so as to not alert any neighbors. Jane led Karen to the bedroom where she had found the kitty behind the mattress and box spring. He seemed quite docile, thank heaven, and Karen scooped him up and put him in the cat carrier. She turned and started to leave. After Karen had taken a few steps, she realized that Jane wasn't following her. She whispered, "Why aren't you leaving too?"

Jane replied, "I'm looking for the food and water dishes I brought here earlier."

An exasperated Karen sharply replied, "Just leave them! We have plenty of those!" Jane replied, "Fingerprints! Fingerprints!"

She immediately gave up her search, and the two left with the cat.

For years afterward, Karen and Jane would mention that nighttime abduction and howl with laughter whenever either one said the word *fingerprints.*

I am told that the cat was named Sir Sweetheart because he was and still is a love muffin. He is still doing very well in his safe home, where he eats all the cat food he wants.

Chapter 28

Jacob and Sigmund

Many times, pet sitters see people who have dogs but not the best environment for them. One pet sitter I know witnessed a family with two children acquire a small black puppy. She talked with the mother of the two children and learned that this dog was a Labrador Retriever and Chow mix. He obviously was going to grow much larger than twenty-five pounds, which would be over the limit allowed by her condo complex.

It was obvious to all observant individuals that this young mother was struggling with two children, a sweet puppy, and a husband who more than once was escorted home by the police because he was caught driving while intoxicated.

The pet sitter watched and worried for several weeks knowing that the puppy was being kept on the outside patio and exposed to the elements. Being a puppy, he was also at risk of digging out of the enclosure and escaping. One time, the sweet one did get out of the enclosure, and she rescued him and took him back home.

She kept watching the family; the husband continued to be escorted home by the police because he had been drinking. She knew this was a bad situation for all concerned.

When the puppy showed up at her doorstep again, she decided that she couldn't in good conscience return the puppy to the family, so she kept him. The young mother stopped by to ask if the puppy had come by her condo again. She said no with an incredibly sincere and straight face that was very hard to manage. She said she didn't like lying but felt that this puppy could escape and get hit by a car or worse. He was solid black.

She asked me if I knew anyone who wanted a puppy. I knew of a young man, a client of mine. He was an established professional with his own home and a large black Labrador whom he adored. He had mentioned to me that he would like to get his buddy, Jake, a companion. So I showed up at his front door one evening after work. I had this small black puppy in my arms and said, "Here's your new puppy."

OMG, you should have seen his face! I knew his heart was melting. This puppy had found a new home. He was named Sigmund, and for several years afterward, I walked Jacob and Sigmund. And Sig did grow up to be an outstandingly handsome sweetheart. At maturity, he was easily sixty to eighty pounds. Jacob was a lab who was nearly the same size. They were beautiful sweethearts.

Chapter 29

Pet Sitters Rescue the World

One evening while I was driving home at ten, I saw the sweet woman whom I had seen walking and lost a few weeks before. I stopped and asked her where she was going. She said that she was looking for her husband. We walked to her home and knocked on her door and rang the doorbell. There was no response.

I suggested that her husband must have stepped out for a bit. I asked her if we could go to a restaurant close by for coffee. I figured that we could wait there for a while and then go back to her home and find her husband there. She was absolutely the sweetest woman on this planet, but I could tell she was anxious to go home.

A half-hour later, I drove her to her house, but still, no one was there. She said that their car was in their parking space, and I wondered if her husband was home but was incapacitated in some way. Having no key, I called the police.

The police came; they seemed familiar with this property and the woman. They knocked and rang the doorbell repeatedly and shouted for the husband to open the door. To my surprise, the husband opened the door. He had been there all along. Evidently, he had poor hearing. It turned out that was not the first time the woman had wandered off.

The police called their daughter to make her aware that this had happened again. Obviously, the police wanted the daughter to get her parents into a safer situation.

My heart went out to all the people involved.

I of course was a kind, law-abiding, good Samaritan who tried to help a lost woman find her way home. I don't want to think what might have happened to her if I hadn't spotted her on the street.

I always stop to pick up a turtle on the street. A few times, I've put the baby beside me and driven to a lake or pond to give it a safe home. I've also stopped to help people round up dogs that have gotten away from them. The most recent case involved a dog that was dodging its owner right in front of their home. The dog thought he was being taken to the vet's office and he wanted no part of that. I had one of my dogs with me. I put her on a leash and walked along the sidewalk. The dog came over to meet my dog, and the owner was able to get the leash on. They appreciated my help.

Chapter 30

Expect Anything

Bailing Gracie Out of Jail

One of my clients has a silver-shaded Persian named Gracie, a sweetheart I have cared for along with her roommates Sophie and Pickles.

On multiple occasions, I have visited the home and cared for everyone, but one time, the owner made an unusual request. She wanted me to bail Gracie out of jail. *What?*

It seemed that a few weeks earlier, Gracie had been taken to the cat groomer to be groomed. Supposedly Gracie had bitten the groomer during the grooming process.

According to Gracie's owner, the groomer must have held a grudge against her or Gracie or both because she reported the incident to Pinellas County Animal Control. Because Grace was not up to date on her vaccinations, she was taken to Pinellas Animal Control and held for observation for rabies.

How ridiculous was that? I knew that rabies vaccinations were for one to three years, but they were effective for six to eight years. Pinellas County and veterinarians there want a steady cash flow at the risk of the health of the county's animals—pure greed comes before the health of our beloved children.

Well, on the appointed day of Gracie's release, I drove to animal control and had her released into my custody. The scenario was ridiculous—a waste of time for everyone. However, people are stupid and sometimes vengeful according to Gracie's owner.

I have to agree. In all the years I have interacted with Gracie and the other siblings in the home, she has never threatened to bite, attack, or do anything else negative. Gracie was a hapless pawn in this exercise in stupidity.

Water Bill Payment

Another time when I visited Gracie's home, I pulled off a notice that had been taped to the front door; the water department wanted some overdue payments or would turn off the water in a day or two.

Well, my client was out of town, so I went to the water department and paid the bill. The animals needed water in the home of course, and the client reimbursed me later.

Thank God for Great Night Vision

One evening, I was driving home and rounded a corner. To my horror, I saw a young woman walking her black cocker spaniel. The young woman was wearing a black skirt. The dog was black, her skirt was black, and the street lights were much too far apart for anyone to walk safely at night. I had to swerve around them to avoid striking them with my vehicle!

I parked in my carport and took my dog, Amy, and a lighted flexi leash and walked over to the young woman. The young woman was very sweet. She was nearly thirty years old and had lived with her brother since her mother had died. This dear soul had Down's syndrome, and she loved her puppy very much. I told her I had almost been unable to see her walking her puppy in the dark. I offered her the lighted flexi leash; I disengaged the leash she had on her dear cocker spaniel, Shadow, and attached the flexi leash. I asked her if she would like to walk a bit with Amy and me. She said yes.

As we were walking, she asked me what church I attended. I told her that I usually didn't go to church because Sundays were prime times for me to take care of my clients' dogs. What she said carved itself in my heart; I'll never forget her words: "I will pray for you. You care for God's creatures."

As I recall this incident, which happened years ago, I am touched as much as I was that evening. She had such a sweet soul. I feel blessed to have taken that walk with her.

Sometimes, others know the greatness of your life's work, or maybe they're put in your path for you to be grateful for the work you do that you love.

Every Day is Unpredictable

photo of disconnection notice

Unexpected things happen and this water bill stating that the water had been shut off is an example of something you may deal with. I have dealt with this issue with other clients as well.

This client had a lovely yellow labrador named Bear. She was sweet as can be and I cared for her many times over the years. On this particular occasion I got to the home and found this. When I walked inside to see Bear I also saw that she had vomited on the carpet in more than one place. Immediately I got paper towels and started cleaning; however, to clean properly I needed water.

Unfortunately, there was no water because of nonpayment of the water bill. This wife was an airline pilot and this husband was a chiropractor. Obviously money was not an issue with them; however, this bill had been overlooked.

I had no choice but to drive down to the City of Safety Harbor's Water Department. I walked in with this and said that I wanted to pay it so that I could take care of Bear who had an upset tummy and I needed to clean the carpet properly.

The lady there recognized me as Nanny Fran who wrote the Ask Nanny Fran Column in The Tropical Breeze Newspaper.

I was very grateful. The comment she wrote touched me, it was incredibly sweet. Thank heaven for small towns where everyone knows everyone in the town.

The note read: As a courtesy to you we turned the water back on, we realize that you are out of town, at the request of dear Nanny Fran on behalf of "Bear".

Chapter 31

Alarms, Locks, and Keys Equal Consternation, Aggravation, and Schedule Slippage

First on my list of aggravating situations is the client who changes his or her locks and forgets to tell you when he or she goes out of town. You get there, the family's gone, and your key won't work. Your only chance of salvation is to try every sliding door, side door, and window to see if you can get inside and care for the sweethearts there.

However, even if you DO succeed you need a way of locking the place up. You have to call the client and inform them about your predicament. In some rare instances, you might find out that the next door neighbor or friend might have the new key, but in 99 percent of the situations, there's no extra key anywhere, and you have to call a locksmith to rekey the front-door lock.

The last time I had this issue, it cost me $70. Homeowners are never happy about that, but it was their fault for not remembering to tell me about the new key.

One time, a family locked me out. The wife had left town first, and when the husband left, he went out the garage door and forgot to undo the burglar latch on the inside of the front door. My key worked fine, but the burglar bar kept me out. I called a locksmith, and we tested all the doors and windows. We found sliding doors that opened out onto the pool area, and one of them wasn't latched. My memory might be dimming on this one; the locksmith might have been able to lift up a sliding door and get it off its tracks. One way or another, I got in.

I called the homeowner about the situation, and he wasn't happy about having left a sliding door unlatched, but that happens at times to all of us on occasion.

Remember the Keys

Another issue is having the keys to the home on your person … at all times! You bet ON YOUR PERSON! One home I was visiting had a front door and back door and a fenced backyard. I went into the home through the front door. I greeted the gorgeous Border Collie sweetheart and we went out into the backyard. On my way out of the kitchen and into the yard, I put my car and the house keys on the kitchen counter. The sweetheart and I played and had a great time.

When I got to the back door, I discovered it had locked on me. It was an older home with an old wiggly lock. Oops, no one told me that this lock was ticklish. So there I was in the backyard with the dog. It was afternoon and I couldn't simply sit outside with this precious sweetheart n the lovely swing hanging from the gorgeous oak tree until the owner got home. Gee, it was a lovely backyard, but I had other animals waiting for me.

I looked around but found no other door or window to the backyard I could open and get into the home through. My logical resort was to go to the side of the house. This yard had an eight-foot chain-link fence all around the yard. On one side of the home, I found a large rubber trash can up against the home. Next to it was an aluminum lawn chair. Just on the other side of the fence was a window with a concrete windowsill. I thought that if I could just hoist my largesse over the fence, I could use the concrete windowsill to step on and then hop to the ground on the other side.

Well, here goes. I moved the lawn chair next to the rubber trash can. I stepped onto the chair and then onto the trash container. The trash barrel was about four feet in height and the lid was approximately three feet in diameter. I had to keep my feet positioned on the outside edges of the trash container because anywhere in the middle would have meant elevator down rapidly. The fence, however, had small triangles of wire jutting up. If I tried to slide my derriere over them, I would suffer nasty scratches, pokes, and rips. So before trying to hoist myself over the fence, I used my shirttail to protect my hand as I bent about a dozen of those wire points down all the while balancing on that garbage can. I had no other choice, I had no plan B.

I was in a very wealthy, old-money, upper-class neighborhood, and I could have been spotted climbing over the fence. All I needed was for the police to show up. I eased my behind over the fence and gingerly extended my foot to the concrete windowsill. I was so happy it was there because otherwise, I would have had to free-fall to the ground from a height of eight feet.

I managed to climb over the fence and gingerly hop off the windowsill to the ground. I walked around to the front door and walked inside. Luckily, I had not been a perfect pet sitter and had not locked the front door when I had first gotten in.

Even if I had kept the keys in my pocket, they wouldn't have helped me in this instance because the old lock on the back door had no key. If I had been super intelligent, I would have checked that out on my way to the backyard. I'm still amazed that not one neighbor saw me climbing over that fence, and I'm still delighted about that as well.

I might have had a cell phone back then. Texting the homeowner may have gotten her attention before a ringing phone if she was occupied with her business. I also realize that without phones having the photo option as they do today, no one was able to record a video of a strange woman climbing out of a backyard that was not hers.

Wow, that photo would have instilled confidence in prospective customers!

Alarms—The Bane of a Pet Sitter's Existence

I have a very embarrassing story to relate here. Usually, alarm systems have a four-digit code that the family inputs to set and turn the alarm off and on. I don't want to know the four-digit codes my clients use. I tell my clients to set up a code just for me, the last four digits of my cell number. That way, I don't have to remember different codes for all the alarm systems I encounter, just the last four digits of my own number.

This very embarrassing incident happened just as I had conceived this idea. This woman was the first client I told to put in the last four digits of my cell phone number for my code. Her kitty needed insulin shots, so getting there every twelve hours was imperative. On top of that, this woman lived in a gated community. At a certain time each evening, the front gates were closed to all but residents. So no matter what had occurred earlier in my day, I had to be inside the gates by eight p.m.—no exceptions

I was nervous about getting through the gates before the bewitching hour. In my nervous state, my mind went numb with panic. I asked myself, *What's the alarm code? I don't remember!* Heavens to Betsy—my first visit, the cat needs a shot, and I can't remember the alarm code. I wanted to make a great impression on this first-time client. I was a nervous wreck before I even approached the gates. I got inside before they closed at eight, but there I was ready to go inside knowing that opening the door would activate the alarm system and the police would come. I was in a state of panic, but that dear kitty needed the insulin shot.

So in I went. I tried a few four-digit codes I thought might work, but of course none did. Eventually, the alarm shut off, and the dear sweet kitty was under the bed hiding. The horrendous scream of the alarm would have shattered anyone's eardrums. Also, this kitty barely knew me. So picture the situation from her viewpoint: *Mom's gone. A stranger is here. There's an awful screeching in my home. Geesh, I'm going to hide.*

That poor dear had been traumatized enough. So I decided to give her some time to calm down without the alarm screeching and then I would crawl under the bed, sweet-talk her, and give her the shot. It was a great plan until the doorbell rang. I stood inside and asked "Who is it?" Well of course it was the police responding to the alarm. You won't believe what I said: "I'm the pet sitter. I don't want to open the door and set the alarm off again. I have to give a scared kitty an insulin shot. Would you mind waiting until I can do that? I'll let you in then."

A very nice officer said, "Ma'am, I understand your dilemma, but I can't just tell my captain that I spoke with a strange woman in this apartment who said she was the pet sitter and then just left."

Even in my stressed-out state, I understood the validity of his statement, so I said, "Okay, come in, but the alarm will screech for few minutes and hurt your eardrums."

I opened the door. He stepped inside. The alarm went off. We stood there for a few minutes with our hands over our ears. When it stopped blaring, he and I talked about my situation. I asked him to wait a few minutes before exiting so I could find the cat and give the shot; I said he and I could leave together. That way, the alarm wouldn't be blaring and hurting eardrums and frightening the kitty again.

He waited while I gave the shot, and we left together.

You think all of that was embarrassing? Standing outside the condo on the street were many neighbors who were walking their dogs or who had come out of their homes to find out why a police car was in their neighborhood. Well, they met the stupid pet sitter. I don't believe I've ever felt so stupid.

I finally got in contact with the homeowner and asked what the alarm code was. She told me that it was the last four digits of my cell number. Oh boy—more *stupid stupid stupid!* After that, I was able to take care of her kitty with no problems, but that was the last time I ever had a client in that neighborhood; everyone told everybody about it.

I'm just human. Unfortunately, my perfectionism had caused me great distress, and if that stress hadn't hit my brain, I might have recalled the new system I had just instituted. Stressing over anything never works. According to Caesar Milan, calm and assertive saves the day panic accomplishes nothing.

Keys

I've had clients in grand homes worth over a million and other clients in much more modest homes. All clients obviously have to give me their house keys to care for their animals. Most clients give me a key and tell me to keep it on file. That way, I'm only a phone call away when they need me to visit their animals. However, other clients want their keys back right away after a job ends. The implication is that they're home and don't trust me anymore to not sneak in and rob them blind. And the clients who are nervous about keys tend to live in modest homes; I feel sorry for them and their paranoia because thieves wouldn't find much of value there. Their furnishings are very similar to the vintage flea market finds in my home.

I'm a professional pet sitter, not a thief. If I were a thief, I'd have a lot more money than I do now. If I ever wanted to break into a house, I could have a key copied and then break into a place whenever I wanted.

More about Alarms

Alarm systems can drive you nuts. And that's particularly the case when you don't know a house even has an alarm system. Yes, that happened to me. In one home, off it went, and I had to call the homeowner to get him to call the alarm company to get it shut off and tell them I wasn't an intruder. That took nearly a day because the home belonged to the man's mother-in-law, who was on vacation. I was able to explain things to the alarm company and not get arrested for breaking and entering. Being the only person in the home with an alarm screaming and the poor animals are petrified stinks! A pet sitter doesn't need to spend time solving problems that could have been avoided in the first place. However, people do screw up.

The strangest alarm situation occurred with a dear client of mine. She had moved from one home to another, and when I went there for the first time when she was out of town, the alarm system went off. She actually knew nothing about the system. I had to call the alarm company and get her on the line—a three-way call. My client explained the situation to the alarm person, and he directed me to a small box on the wall of her bedroom. He told me to open it and unscrew some connections. Then he directed me to the garage. He instructed me to look up. Attached to the ceiling was another plastic box. I needed a ladder to get to it and unscrew a few more connections. I reassured the man that I did know the difference between a flat head and a Phillips screwdriver and understood his instructions.

My client complimented me on my knowledge and abilities. She evidently hadn't wired an entire house or built furniture from scratch as I had. I loved this woman, but I couldn't spend that much time there because I had other babies waiting for me elsewhere. However I did spend the extra time because there was no other choice. She never reimbursed me for the extra time I had spent at her home that day. It simply never occurred to her to do so.

In fact, not one client has ever given me extra compensation for the extraordinary time involved to sort out their alarm problems. People don't think. I am there. They know that they are paying me to be there. End of story. However, maybe I spent a total of two or three hours to resolve a problem. People have never taken the extra time into consideration.

Lights Out

Power outages can affect a home and even kill the babies inside. Always pay attention to stormy weather. Besides worrying about Fido shivering, shaking, and whining because he is fearful of thunder and lightning, you also need to worry if the client has an aquarium filled with fish.

One evening, I went to a home and fed nearly forty animals. Nine dogs had to go out to tinkle in the backyard and then be let back in to be fed. Then the cats had to have fresh food and water put out for them, and their litter boxes needed to be cleaned. Nearly a dozen food dishes needed to be cleaned and refilled with wet food, and then six litter boxes needed to be cleaned, and finally, one kitten needed drops in her ears.

With all that done, I picked up my keys and phone. As I approached the front door, all the lights went out. I needed my phone's flashlight feature to lock the front door. Then I noticed that all the homes on the street had lost their electricity. Well, all the animals had everything they needed except for light, so I left the home.

I drove away and went to another home that had kitties to care for. After that, I drove to the blacked-out neighborhood. I saw people standing in a driveway and emergency vehicles farther up the street. I stopped to ask what had happened and learned that two transformers had blown up and that electrical lines were down. Nasty. I went to the home where I was staying overnight. Thank heaven it wasn't involved in the power outage.

Speaking of electricity, I need it in the morning to make coffee. I desperately need it to make coffee. Because some homes I stay in don't have coffee makers or they have those Keurig things I don't know how to operate and are worried about breaking, I bring along my simple-to-operate Mr. Coffee.

I cannot think of any animals that could be injured or killed because of lack of electricity except for snakes if the air conditioning is off for a long time and a home becomes very hot. Snakes can and will die in the heat. Heat lamps on other creatures will turn off, and in a cold climate, certainly most of them could die without the heat lamp. And fish could die if a pump stops working for a long time.

For this reason—a power outage—pet sitters need keys to doors, not just garage door openers as some clients want to give pet sitters; they don't work without power. So always get a key as a backup to a garage door opener in case of an outage. That way, you'll be able to get in and get out and lock the place up.

Another good tip for pet sitters is to know and AVOID the low-lying areas and roads that can flood in a heavy downpour. A pet sitter does not need water that is high enough to stall the engine and make brakes useless. If you cannot use your vehicle you will need to instantly acquire alternate transportation. In most instances that is not possible.

Chapter 32

Those Are Mean Streets Out There

Helpers have to be trained. I took a lovely woman, Linda, with me to see two beautiful dogs, Cisco and Deja. This was a home that I had visited several times before, so I expected no problems with this training session.

We walked up to the front door, went inside, and headed straight to the control panel for the alarm system. I quickly entered the code the family had given me, but it didn't take. I believe I entered it too quickly and messed up the system. Well, this incredible siren goes off and I cannot stand it!

Eventually, it shut off, and the alarm company called the home phone. Of course I knew who it was, so I answered. I told the company that I was the pet sitter, that I had entered the code too quickly for the system, and that it hadn't taken.

The alarm company person asked me if I knew the password. I believe the person at the alarm company told me that it was one of their dog's names. I replied, "Then it's either Cisco or Deja." They wouldn't let that be a satisfactory response even when I told them I could give them the husband's and wife's cell phone numbers and that they could be reached in Orlando. They said they were sending the police to check out the home. I replied, "Come on over."

I told Linda, "Let's walk the dogs. When we get back, the police will be here."

We leashed Cisco and Deja and went for our walk. After the walk, we approached the home and saw two police officers outside. Linda and I had to pass my car as we approached the home. I reached in and grabbed one of my business cards. I held the card in my hand at the end of my outstretched arm at eye level and announced to the officers that I was the pet sitter.

One officer was definitely all business and scowled at me during the entire time he was on the property. The other stood behind him and seemed to have a pleasant countenance but definitely wasn't smiling either, but I do believe I saw intermittent twinkles coming from her eyes.

Linda and I were both on the other side of forty-five, and I was five feet-five inches tall and Linda was all of five feet tall. We were two Caucasian women walking two beautiful dogs who were quite at ease with us.

However, none of that put even a hint of a smile on his face or changed his gruff tone. He was impersonating an ICE agent, a know-it-all bully. He said, "I'll need to go inside and check out the home." Again, not a hint of a smile. Mr. I'm Mean and Angry was making a statement. Definitely he was an ICE agent (obviously a time traveler from the year 2019).

I said, "I'm sure the homeowners will be relieved to have you check out their home." I could have said, "Forget that nonsense," but then, Linda and I could have been tossed into the paddy wagon.

We went into the home and walked into the kitchen, which was long and narrow with a fifteen-foot long island in the center. We were all standing in the kitchen. The policeman who wanted to check out the whole house for a break-in didn't do that. He looked at his female partner and visually surveyed the area. They stood on one side of the island while Linda and I were on the opposite side.

I had previously placed my can of Mace on the waist-high kitchen island and had forgotten about it in all the confusion of the alarm, the call from the alarm company, and the police coming to investigate. And it was a large can of Mace with the words *Policeman's Model* on it. I noticed the male police officer was eyeballing it; he asked if it was mine. I replied that it was. I could tell he was expecting some sort of explanation.

I looked at him with eyes wide open and stated, "Those are mean streets out there." Wouldn't you expect nearly every person in the room to burst out laughing? Most especially the two officers? As if I were telling them something they didn't already know.

Not one word came from the male officer, but the female officer was giving off the tiniest beginning of a smile, and her eyes were twinkling like Disneyland at night. I swear she wanted to burst out laughing. This entire scenario was so patently ridiculous. Linda and I were obviously two women pet-care providers who had accidently set off the alarm—end of story.

The officers said they were leaving and admonished us to secure the home properly when we exited. Well, officers, I assure you with you here or not here, we would definitely secure the home as we left. We *are* professional pet sitters after all.

As Linda and I were giving water, treats, and love to Cisco and Deja, we couldn't stop laughing. She couldn't get over the pompous male officer, and neither could I. We bade goodnight to Cisco and Deja, secured the home, and left. All the way home, Linda was laughing. She thought it was hysterical when I opened my car door to grab one of my business cards and held it up in the air as I walked towards the officers stating, "I'm the pet sitter." I must have sensed from many feet away that Mr. Pompous Nasty Pants was going to relate only to a serious, bona-fide, pet-care professional, and I wanted him to have no doubt about my identity.

Linda and I giggled and laughed all the way home. Linda grew up in NYC and had witnessed police officers and terrible crimes more than I cared to imagine. With that background, she was nearly rolling on the floor with laughter at the entire encounter with Mr. Pompous Nasty Pants. Hey, I'm an Indiana farm girl. The worst thing that ever happened in my small town was my high school friends tipping over outhouses on Halloween night. But even with my Rebecca of Sunny Brook Farm childhood, I too was breathless with laughter.

Neither Linda nor I will ever forget Mr. Pompous Nasty Pants or the gentle and quiet female officer who accompanied him and didn't utter a word. She was very wise.

Chapter 33

Some Homes You Just Love

I've fallen in love with many of the homes I've been in because they are unique, cozy, full of life, bright, and cheerful or because I like the folks who live there. The energy of the lovely people who occupy those homes has permeated their homes, and I enjoy that loving energy when I visit.

I brought up this subject because I nearly burned down one of the homes I dearly loved. Thank heaven I'm not a pet sitter who runs in and out of a home as quickly as possible because if I had done that, the home I'm talking about would have gone up in flames.

I cared for four incredibly sweet and loving kitties in one home, so being there was always a joy. The woman who lived there was warm, loving, eclectic, happy … well, you know—I just liked and admired her.

On one particular visit, I was in the kitchen preparing wet and dry kitty food and washing and refilling the water dishes. Just outside the kitchen was a closet where the woman had stored a large bag of dry cat food. I reasoned that it would be more convenient if it were in the kitchen along with the wet food and dishes. I took it to the kitchen and put it on the stove toward the back.

I went about my duties while loving the kitties, and then I checked on the litter boxes. When I returned to the kitchen, I saw smoke near the ceiling. At first, I thought that the ceiling fan was on fire. While my mind was racing trying to think of how to shut off the electricity to stop the fan, I turned and saw that the cat food bag on the stove was smoking greatly. I realized that I must have bumped one of the burner controls on when I pushed the bag toward the back of the stove. The bag was burning! I pulled the bag off the stove onto the floor and turned the knob to the off position. I cleaned up the half-burned bag and saved most of the cat food. My heart started beating again, and oxygen returned to my brain. I thanked God over and over that I had been there to witness the smoke and potential fire. I loved the kitties, the woman, and the home, and I would have been devastated if I had caused the home to burn down.

I was so grateful that I always tried to spend as much time as possible with the animals and not rush in and out.

Chapter 34

Dogs Chew Things

One of my clients who lived in an apartment had two dogs, sweet young pups. One was a huskie, and the other was a sweet brown and black dog. I visited the apartment three times daily to walk them. Since they were so young, they were full of energy, and whenever I walked into the apartment, I could count on things having been pulled off the kitchen counter, the trash can explored, and its contents lying all around the kitchen. After you have visited young and active pups for years, few things surprise you. However, I did get a big surprise on the second or third evening I went to walk the two pups.

While I had been away, they had gone into their father's bedroom and gotten hold of several of his pornographic DVDs. Oops! I did my best to gather up all the cases and DVDs I found lying all around the living room, and I went into the master bedroom; it was obvious where the pups had found the collection. I did my best to put them back in the original cabinet. I closed the bedroom door, and we took our walk.

Chapter 35

Television Is On and No One's Home

One home I had to visit had two dogs to walk. They were very sweet, and the walks went well. I was shocked though one morning when we got back from a walk; I saw that the three of us had tracked in some dirt, so I searched for a vacuum cleaner. I opened the door to a bedroom and was shocked to see a very large screen TV on—two naked people were having sex. I had no idea what was going on. There was supposed to be no one home. That was why I had been hired to walk the dogs. I shut the door and said goodbye to the dogs. I never opened the door again on following visits. So much for trying to tidy up after yourself.

That was a shock to my system at seven in the morning, when I'm never fully awake. In all my years of visiting homes, that happened only once thank heaven.

Chapter 36

A Day in the Life of Felony Frannie

I got up one morning to walk my two dogs. I have two horseshoe-shaped streets to walk on, and I chose to walk on the street I didn't live on. I was looking at the buildings around me as usual. I watched for anything unusual, usually regarding animals more than people, and I saw a raccoon trapped in a cage underneath a condo carport. I felt so sorry for the raccoon; however, with two dogs in tow, I was in no position to do anything about it.

I walked my dogs home and found a pair of leather gloves. Having grown up on the farm and knowing wild animals as I did, I knew better than to approach an unhappy, mistakenly trapped wild creature without leather gloves.

I got into my car and drove back to the building. When I arrived, an SUV pulled into the same carport. I sprang into action. I approached the young woman who was exiting the vehicle. She was on her cell phone talking to animal control. She asked me if I was with animal control. I replied, "No, I'm with SPOT USA." She continued to speak with animal control. I volunteered to release the raccoon back into the woods and save animal control a trip to Palm Harbor. That seemed fine with everyone involved; the woman ended her conversation with animal control.

I opened the back end of my vehicle and lifted the poor dear into it. I drove to my street, which backs up to a wooded area. I pulled as close as possible to the wooded area and carried the cage with the frightened raccoon toward the woods. Thank heaven for my leather gloves as the raccoon was entirely out of patience with the ordeal; he was growling and attacking my hand whenever it went near the cage.

I managed to unclip the clip that secured the trap door of the cage, but I was fearful of opening it with him or her so unhappy; I feared I might be attacked. Well, I was wearing shorts and sandals though I was wearing leather gloves. This is Florida, remember? I didn't fear that the raccoon was rabid, but I didn't want to chance an attack. I thought if the critter threw his body weight against the door, it would be free. Since I was unsure if the door operated in that fashion, I decided to go away and come back later to check on the creature. If need be, I'd devise a way to hoist the door up to release the dear one.

I drove home and answered my cell phone. I had previously given my number and name to the young woman in the SUV, who had in turn passed it on to animal control. I hadn't been able to answer immediately, so I retrieved my voice mail. Voice mail was quite gruff—call this number at once! Achtung! I did, and the person who answered was doing his best to intimidate this innocent taxpayer. I was grilled, really grilled: "Did you take one of our traps with a wild animal in it and release the animal?"

"Yes, I took the trap, but I haven't released the animal."

The achtung, let's make this citizen tinkle in her frillies attitude and tone of voice informed me, "Do you know that you will be arrested and charged as a felon because you have stolen Pinellas County property and released a wild animal that was indeed the property of Pinellas County Animal Control?"

I replied, "No of course not. I was not aware of that."

I was ordered immediately, posthaste, STAT, to take said raccoon in said cage to an animal control officer who was waiting for me at the crime scene.

I said I indeed would do as he asked. I shucked off my shorts and sandals and got into heavy-duty jeans and rugged hiking boots. I wanted whomever I was about to meet to understand that I knew the dangers of a frightened raccoon who could do major harm to anyone in his or her path if the mood struck. I may have been a felon, but I wasn't an idiot.

I'm a dumb blonde, but dumb blondes and felons are mutually exclusive categories of people. What do you think?

I drove to the crime scene, and there was the animal control truck. I pulled next to it and got out to walk around to greet the officer with a big smile on my face and bright demeanor. I asked with a big smile and an outstretched hand, "Hello! How are you?" I explained that I worked with various rescue organizations and was familiar with this trap. I said that I of course had recognized that this poor dear raccoon had accidently been trapped in the cage and that I had just wanted to release it back into the wild.

This male officer wanted some identification. I replied that I didn't have my driver's license with me. He gave me a surprised look. I said, "I live here." I didn't think I needed my purse (which contained my driver's license) to drive around the corner in this complex. His look said, *Uh, I understand that.*

I pulled out the latest copy of the *Tropical Breeze* newspaper from my car and opened it to page 24, which contained my "Ask Nanny Fran" column. I told him Nanny Fran was me. I pointed to my name, number and email listed there and said I'd been a professional pet sitter in the county for fourteen years. I explained that I'd started writing my column to help educate people in ways to assure the health, safety, and long life of their beloved pets. He and I started exchanging war stories about people being thoughtless, clueless, and careless about their pets. We quickly developed a mutual respect for each other and our careers. He told me that usually, people try to free such caged animals so they can steal the cage—costly for the county—and the courts had ruled it a felony to do that. Hence, I could have faced a felony theft charge and become Felony Frannie instead of Nanny Frannie.

But our few minutes of chatting engendered an empathetic understanding between both parties concerning our mutual animal-welfare endeavors and concerns. I suggested that he follow me to the cage, and he did. When we reached a stop sign, I saw Pat, my fellow animal lover and friend. She had seen my vehicle followed closely by the animal control truck. Her quirky, smart-ass smile spoke volumes. Pat knew me very well. I said, "Get in. I'll fill you in on the way." Brave soul that she is, she did. We drove a block or so, and I pulled into the parking area that backed up to the wild area.

The animal control officer pulled in too. I got out to speak with the young man. We saw the poor dear raccoon still in the cage. I said, "I was going to release him as I've heard of no rabies concerns in the county for quite some time. However, I understand you may have to take this dear one back to the county to be killed."

He opened one of the side doors on his truck and retrieved a wire cage that contained a young opossum. He set it on the ground. He said something like, "Well, gee— somehow the opossum escaped." He opened the cage. The baby opossum skittered off into the wild area. He and I were smiling ear to ear. I was overjoyed to see him do that with that innocent critter he had dutifully picked up from a trap.

He walked to that dear raccoon and lifted the gate. Another of God's precious little ones skittered off into the wild area. Wow! I asked him if I could give him a hug and kiss—on his cheek. His smile was sheepish, sweet, and boyish. His eyes were beaming with happiness and pride as I gave him a hug and that kiss on his cheek. And Pat was beaming a sweet smile too!.

I told her a story this young man had told me minutes earlier about a woman who had been reported for not caring properly for her five young pit bull puppies in her backyard.

He checked on the condition of the animals, and the owner informed him that she had given them fresh water and food that morning. He asked to see the dogs. When he saw the poor puppies walking in their feces, water dishes lined with green slime, and food dishes with maggots crawling over the food, he told her he would have to give her citations for each puppy—$118 each.

She protested, and he said, "Ma'am, I don't want to have to write five separate citations. They have seven layers of paper, and I'll have to press hard. I don't want to issue you these citations." He said he wouldn't give her any citations if she would drink from the dogs' water dish and eat from the bowl.

She said, "Take the dogs."

He had taken five beautiful bluenose pit bull puppies to animal control, and each was adopted out to a new home.

My friend listened to his story with wide-eyed disbelief not at his story but at the idea anyone would treat dogs that way—so neglectfully.

He said he was constructing an area in his backyard so he could take fear-aggressive dogs home with him to be rehabilitated. He said he could work with a dog for three weeks and take away the fears that fueled any aggressive tendencies. God bless him. He was committed to giving these dear ones a second chance.

He said he was working toward a special certification that would allow him to work with wildlife such as snakes and other wildlife. He planned to someday go to Puerto Rico and set up an animal shelter on the island. I asked him to give me a call. I told him that I was writing books and that one of them would be about people like himself who were going the extra mile to save animals, people who were caring for animals with their hearts and their own money. I told him I was honored to have met him, and I was. We said our goodbyes.

By the way, he didn't charge me with a felony.

Nasty Pants Again

Pat and I were in my condo discussing the spaying and neutering we were planning for a feral mother kitty and her four kittens when my cell phone rang.

Again, it was animal control. This Nasty Pants, I'm In Control Officer, proceeded to question me about me NOT vaccinating my dog. When I had first met with the first young man I had told him of the dangers of vaccinations and then I was presumed to be a lawbreaker because of said conversation!

I immediately informed the officer that my dog had died January 2nd at the age of 15 after a four year battle with cancer.

I immediately went into my best tearful performance of loss of my pet so that this Annoying Brainless County Employee would GET OFF MY CASE! Damn it all … vaccinate and kill … it is all about money … not saving lives!

Well, it worked. I am a very convincing actress. However, between you and me, whenever I speak of losing my dear Amy (my only reason for drawing a breath) the acting is not acting.

Well, when I heard a very solicitous, "Oh, I am so very sorry. Wow, you had her 15 years! Well, you did right by her! I replied thank you."

Then I told her about the Ask Nanny Fran newspaper column I wrote. Possibly the young man who had just left my condominium complex had called in to report that all was well and that he had not charged me.

I presume that he also told his "superior" that I was a well-known local figure and that I could be contacted via internet, phone, etc. with the information printed at the bottom of my column.

Ergo, the question, how do I get to your column on the internet? I explained to the officer on the phone how to navigate the Tropical Breeze web site to find the Ask Nanny Fran column. I stated that I wrote the column to help people to understand instinctual feline and canine behavior so that animals might not be given up to shelters so readily.

The officer on the other end commended me for writing to educate the general populace. The conversation ended with well wishes on both ends.

When I got off the phone I looked at Pat and said, "You know, I bet that the main reason this officer wanted to look at my web site was because I told the young man about the dangers of vaccinations!"

It is totally amazing that in the space of say an hour and half that I go from being public enemy number one who is to be charged with a felony to the greatest and most compassionate animal lover on the planet.

And all of this would never have happened if I had not taken my dogs for a walk this morning!

This happened in 2008. However, while reading it again it feels as though I am there with this lovely young man and my dear friend.

Chapter 37

A Really Big Oops

I have made mistakes many times, but thank heaven I can laugh about them when I retell the stories. I don't know if there's a sadomasochistic tendency in me that relishes reliving the pain of total embarrassment or what.

Actually, I find what I manage to do incredibly funny and want to make people laugh about that. Most people dread appearing foolish. Obviously, I am not one of those people. I want people to know that no one is perfect and that laughing about their "oops" is healthy for the psyche.

One time when I was driving on a busy highway, I answered my cell phone. The call was from a woman who wanted me to care for her kitty while she was away. I kept driving while talking as the road was jammed with cars and it was going to be nearly a life-altering event to maneuver into the far lane and pull off the roadway. I made an appointment to meet her and her kitty that afternoon. She told me what apartment complex she lived in, and I knew very well where it was, but since I was driving, I couldn't write down her apartment number. I thought I could remember it if I repeated it enough times.

Since this woman had only one kitty, I thought I would let Nanny Alice be the caregiver. I always gave Alice, a retiree, kitties to visit because I didn't want her being pulled down a sidewalk by a large dog; those I kept for myself. I've been pulled six ways from Sunday by dogs for twenty-six years. I've even tripped over my feet and fallen flat on the sidewalk in front of everyone in the neighborhood. However, that's okay because I'm young and tough.

Alice and I went to the apartment complex and went to the apartment whose number was indelibly imprinted in my brain. I knocked on the door, and a young man with some kind of Spanish accent greeted us. I said, "We're here for our appointment." I was standing there all smiles and so was Alice. Who would be concerned about a sweet, forty-year-old young woman who was all smiles and a salt-and-pepper haired woman in her sixties? This young man seemed a bit confused, and in broken English, he said he would get his wife. When a lovely young woman came to the door, I smiled, extended my hand, and stated, "I'm here for our appointment."

The woman graciously invited us in. Alice and I stepped in and met two young children and a dog. My God he was darling! He was Benji cute! However, he was shy around strangers. I knew what to do; I lay down on the floor. I was on my back, my knees were bent, my feet were together, and my hands were on my chest. I told Nanny Alice, "This is the international symbol in dog language that means I'm entirely submissive and won't hurt you." I was hoping the dog would come over, sniff me, wag its tail, and immediately become my best friend.

Well, the dog knew something was strange and stayed at the opposite end of the living room. I looked like a complete fool. However, looking like a complete fool and actually realizing that you have been a complete fool are two different things; the latter prompts total embarrassment.

I had an epiphany. I asked the young woman, "You don't have a cat do you?"

"No I don't," she said.

There I was lying on her floor. I felt absolutely ridiculous. Sheepishly, I got up off the floor and asked the woman if I could telephone the woman we were supposed to meet. She said of course, so I called the woman and asked her for her apartment number. She told me, and I told her that I was next door to her in her neighbor's apartment and would be at her door in a few moments. My future client said she hadn't met the family living next door. "Would you like an introduction?" I asked with a huge smile.

Alice and I thanked the woman and her family for allowing us to come in and introduce ourselves, and we walked two or three steps to the neighbor's door. That time, we had the correct apartment.

After our meeting, Alice and I got in my jeep and drove away. Oh my God, we were laughing until our sides were aching! We knew how ridiculous we looked to have not only knocked on the wrong door but also going inside and my getting on the floor of a stranger's apartment. I had made a complete fool of myself.

Alice and I hoped that we would never look that ridiculous ever again.

Chapter 38

Happy Valentine's Day Everyone!

Flowers everywhere and I love them. However, I cannot bring them into my home unless they're kept in my refrigerator because my kitties think they are edible. I'll stash one rose or a small bouquet in my refrigerator, so whenever I open the door, my eyes will enjoy their beauty and my nose will revel in the fragrance. I'll put the small bouquet or single rose beside my plate when I eat.

I've been a professional pet sitter for many years, and I've enjoyed beautiful flowers in other homes. In February one year, I was scheduled to visit a lovely woman's three fur children several times daily while she was away on business. Shortly after she left town, she called me and said she had just been made aware that a dozen long-stemmed roses had been delivered to her front door. She was already on her way to the airport; she kindly said, "You enjoy them. They'll be dead by the time I return."

When I arrived at her home, I found the roses, put them in a vase, and set them on her table. I then loved, played with, and walked her two adorable fur children. After returning from our walk, I took the roses and put them on the floor of my car between the two front seats. I thought I was brilliant. With the AC running for most of the day, I figured the roses would fare quite nicely and I could enjoy them for several days.

While I was driving to my next stop, I thought, *The roses were a totally unexpected bit of pleasure for me, so why not share them? After all, it's Valentine's Day!*

I stopped and purchased a simple card that stated something akin to "Thank you for being you. You are very special."

I drove to Walmart, where a dear friend of mine was working, but I learned she was on break just then. A few minutes later, my friend returned. I gave her a hug and told her I had something for her in my car. As I was walking to my car, I saw a young woman having no luck trying to fit a bicycle she had just purchased into her car. I drive a full-size van with only the two front seats in place. The remainder of the van is always ready to accommodate three Great Danes, six Border Collies, or ten Maltese ... you get the picture. I told the young woman that she could put her bike in my van—plenty of room—and I would follow her to her house, which I figured was nearby. She said she lived only a few blocks away. I said, "Wonderful! Put your bike in my car. I'll be right back."

I grabbed a rose and the card and ran back to my friend. I wished her a happy Valentine's Day, and she beamed and gave me a big hug.

I got back to my van and told the woman I'd follow her home. When we got there, I unloaded her new bicycle and we chatted for a minute or two. She told me she was a single mom of a teenage daughter. The woman's previous bicycle had been stolen. She said she had decided to purchase another bike with her paycheck before every dollar disappeared into the normal bill-paying routine. She told me that riding her bicycle was her daily stress relief. I was touched by her and her story. I reached into my van and plucked one red rose from my bouquet. I handed it to her and wished her a happy Valentine's Day. Her lovely smile spoke volumes, and I was filled with joy.

I drove off and went back to the Walmart to see my friend. I had rushed out so quickly that I wanted to go back. She had no children or family, she didn't drive, and she was extremely worried then about her dear husband's health. I felt she needed to know that others were watching over her and caring for her.

When I arrived back at the store, she grinned from ear to ear and gave me a huge hug. She had put the rose in a glass she had gotten from the sandwich shop in the store; someone there had cut the stem down a bit. Talk about proud ... talk about happy ... talk about a beautiful smiling face radiating pure joy. I was filled with a happiness I cannot describe except to state that it was blissful.

I drove to another friend's home and stopped in unexpectedly. I gave her a rose as well and wished her a happy Valentine's Day. After that, I gassed up at my regular gas station. Behind the counter was a gentleman who was always pleasant with me. My gut feeling was that he'd go home that evening and would be the only person there. I slipped back out to my car and came in with a rose. I handed it to him with an impish smile and stated, "Your secret admirer asked me to deliver this rose to you and made me promise not to tell you her name. Happy Valentine's Day!"

Two mornings later, the woman with the three fur children arrived home just after I had taken her sweethearts for their walk. I hadn't expected her to be home so early in the day; she had told me that she would be home several hours later and that the young man who had sent the roses would be coming home with her. She asked me where the roses were. I nearly fainted as I had totally not expected that to happen, but I smiled with an assured air of calmness and told her I would bring them to her.

Thank heaven I had not given all of them away. They actually looked quite nice as I knew how to care for cut flowers. I produced maybe eight or nine beautiful long-stemmed red roses for her to place in full view of her boyfriend when he got there. Yikes! How incredible it was that I hadn't given all the roses away in twelve grand gestures of kindness and friendship.

Chapter 39

Golden Lion Needs New Home

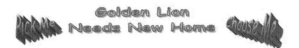

Four-Year-Old Chow and Golden Retriever Mix

Barkley's previous owner died, and he needs to find a forever home quickly. Great with kids of all ages. He would prefer to be the only pet in your home.

This wonderful young fellow weighs eighty-four pounds. He's very smart and sweet and will be the perfect pet for someone who understands and loves chows!

Please contact Francene, the owner of Never Say Goodbye Pet Sitting. FranAndAmy@gmail.com

One day in December 2007, I was in shock and disbelief. Don had died the previous day. I wondered about Barkley, his and my beautiful sweetheart. I'd been Don's pet sitter and friend for four years, and Barkley's future was up for grabs. I was so concerned about him.

A client of mine had called me the previous evening and told me that her daughter had seen an ambulance and police cars at Don's home earlier in the day. I saw no reason for the police to also be there unless there had been foul play. Since his neighborhood was an upper-middle-class neighborhood, I didn't expect that. My creative imagination was worried beyond belief that Don had become ill and had called 911.

When the rescuers came to administer aid to him, they encountered Barkley, who I thought might have tried to protect his best friend. Woe is me. I won't go on with my thoughts about what might have happened. God had Don in his care, and I hoped both were watching over dear Barkley and making sure he was being cared for properly.

I knew Don quite well. I admired and respected him and enjoyed his company. He went to heaven in his early sixties, very young. I was sixty-one then, and I felt younger than even some thirty-year-olds; walking dogs keeps you physically active and optimistic and cheerful!

I talked every day with my eighty-four-year-old aunt Mary; she and I are carbon copies of one another. She lived by herself in the most wonderful Victorian home in Point of Rocks, Maryland. God bless her. So Don's death at his age shocked me.

My greatest concern then was Barkley, who in spite of his wonderful nature would be difficult to place in a new home. I couldn't take him in due to rules and regulations as to the number and size of animals allowed in my home. Shhhh, yeah, I know the rules!

Barkley loved everyone big and small. He adored children, and he wasn't interested in other dogs. I thought he considered himself a two-legged individual rather than a dog. But Mr. B or Barks as I often referred to him had always been a cat chaser, so he couldn't be placed in a home with a cat. And most people are afraid of even fifty-pound dogs, and there he was at eighty-four pounds.

He had the most gorgeous, long, golden coat. Grooming him entailed anesthetizing him so he could be shaved down once or twice a year. That's how Don cared for this sweet fellow; it was time consuming, but Barks was definitely worth every second. He was a sweetheart, and his father and I loved him. I would have hated for him to be euthanized without having been given a chance to be adopted into another loving home. I prayed, *Dear God, please do your best for my sweet Barkley. Thank you.*

After a very worried night, I cared for my dear ones, showered, and went on the road with my miracle child, HRH Amelia Elizabeth. I stopped at the bank and then at Munchies Pet Food Store for some wonderful wet dog food that my sweetheart seemed to like as well as Fancy Feast cat food. That was saying something; cat food usually beats out all contenders. When I come upon very good quality wet dog food she likes, I rush to acquire more of it.

I then drove by Don's home. I saw no signs of life. I drove to his daughter's home. She had just driven to Tampa's airport to pick up her mother, Don's ex, who had just flown in from Canada. She had asked me to stop by because she had wanted to talk to me. I of course wanted to talk with her and offer assistance with Barkley or anything else she needed. She and I hugged tightly. I told her how sorry I was to hear about Don.

The poor dear was only forty. She had been quite concerned about her father's health for the previous few years. Don had been in and out of the hospital over the past couple of years and had been seeing a doctor regularly for heart and blood conditions. However, each time I met Don, he was always upbeat, cheerful, and very pleasant.

I gave my condolences to her, her mother, and her husband, and I asked about Barkley. I needed to know if he was fine and what the plan was for him. I learned that on Monday morning, Don had given Barkley his walk and that later in the day when his son-in-law had gone to walk Barkley, he had found Don lying dead on the bedroom floor.

Barkley was being kept at Don's home; his daughter and her husband were driving over there to walk him daily. I asked if I could stop by and give him attention and walk him when I had the time. They said of course.

Barkley obviously knew something was very different. I wanted to be able to love him and spend some time with him so he wouldn't grieve alone over his best friend. Don and I were Barkley's world as Don's daughter and husband had their own home, puppies, and lives.

Don's daughter said that they were planning on fencing in their yard at their home and possibly making some changes in their home for Barkley. They had two small dachshunds; one was very friendly and outgoing while the other was shy. Barkley had been raised an only child and would need to be properly introduced to the new dogs so he wouldn't consider them threats or become jealous of them.

I offered to help them acquire the services of a canine behaviorist to offer assistance if needed. I knew Barkley inside and out; getting him adjusted to two small dogs would take effort, and we needed to do it correctly the first time out of the gate.

Don had a group of friends he corresponded with regularly via email, me included. One of his friends had contacted the others on the list about Don's death. It was a very heartwarming experience to read what Don's friends of many years had to say about the unexpected news. Everyone mentioned that Don had always been a pleasant, upbeat, dear friend and a consummate professional as a sports broadcaster. I printed out the emails so his daughter could read them; I thought that reading the glowing tributes people around the country and Canada had written about her father would help her. I was happy she was married and didn't have to deal with her father's demise on her own. I was also pleased that her mother came to help deal with all the arrangements. And of course I was happy that Barkley had a home and would not be taken to the vet to be put down or taken to the animal shelter.

I had wondered if the last time I had seen Barkley the previous Friday would be the last time I would ever see him. That Friday was the last time I saw Don. I was so glad that we had a pleasant conversation, but we always did. I liked Don. He had a great sense of humor. He was always upbeat. I admire people like that. It takes great inner strength and will to always be upbeat and cheerful, but I think there's no better way to be.

A few days later, I stopped by Don's home to spend some time with Barkley. As I pulled into Don's driveway, a man pulled in there as well. He introduced himself as a longtime friend of Don's. He gave me his business card, and I told him I would give it to Don's daughter and son-in-law.

Barkley and I had a wonderful time together. I took him to the locksmith with me as I needed to duplicate a key. While there, he received lots of attention from the owner of the shop and his three sons. Barks needed that.

I took him to Philippe Park, and we walked and walked. I let him lead the way as much as possible but steered him away from other dogs and dog walkers. Just as we were leaving, a young father with a child in tow approached us. The wee one wanted to pet the puppy though this puppy weighed over eighty pounds, an intimidating size.

I reassured the father that Barkley adored people and especially wee ones. Well, true to form, Barkley did his usual. He lay down flat on the ground so the wee one would not be intimidated by his size. I stood there petting Barkley along with the child, and Barks loved every minute.

We said goodbye, and I took Barkley home. I stopped by Don's daughter's home to give her that business card from Don's longtime friend. Melanie told me that they were going to fly to Canada, where Don would have a memorial service and a viewing. I asked about the care of their two dachshunds and Barkley while they were gone, and she said they would be boarding Barkley and their dogs. I was horrified. I said that Barkley had never been boarded. They said that the boarding facility had a canine behaviorist on staff. I walked away very upset. I don't care whose dog you and I are speaking of—boarding is not an option. I had heard so many horror stories about boarding that I would never board any dog of mine particularly over holidays, when substitutes often take over for the regular staff. I refused to allow my mind to travel where it was straining at the leash to go regarding all the horrific events that could happen with Mr. B at one of those facilities.

Even though it was New Year's, I offered to walk Barks for free while they were gone. I had no idea how long they would be gone, but I couldn't bear to think of what might happen to Barkley in a kennel. I hoped that free pet sitting would appeal to them.

I told a fellow pet sitter about all this; she had walked him when I hadn't been able to. She was appalled. Someone else suggested that Don may not have left his daughter much money, and I remember Melanie being concerned about $500 to get her passport renewed though she'd be staying with her mother and therefore not have hotel costs.

On Christmas Day, I went over to Barkley's home at five p.m. to pick him up, but he wasn't there. I panicked. I was afraid he had become ill and had been rushed to the emergency vet. I rushed to Melanie and

Bill's home. When I walked to the door, I heard Barkley bark. He was in the garage! I tried the door, and it was unlocked. No one was home.

I scribbled a note that I had come to take Barkley to the park as usual and taped it to the door. I took Barkley to the park, and we walked all around for an hour. When he wanted to sit, we sat. I took all the time he wanted.

On the way home, I stopped by Barkley's old home to see if all his food and treats had been taken to the new home; they had been. He wanted to walk around the old neighborhood. He went into the front yard and sat facing the street. I thought, *Sweet dear, you're permanently affixing that scene in your memory. You know that your life is changing.*

We ambled up the sidewalk. I let him lead the way and set the pace. Somehow, I knew it was our last walk in the neighborhood we knew so well. When we got to the end of the street, we sat on the grass. On the opposite side of the street was a home with a Christmas display of lights and music. Barks and I were alone in the cool of the night. I don't know how long we sat there, but finally, I told him we had to get moving.

We walked back to his home, but he wanted to walk farther. We went around the cul-de-sac and back. It was as if he wanted to travel every inch of sidewalk he and I had traveled several hundred times. I felt he know it was his final walk in his old neighborhood. It was a mournful walk for me. I knew that Melanie and Bill wouldn't be traveling as much as Don had, so my visits with Barkley would be few and far between. I was quite sad. Our relationship would come to an end.

I had him jump in my car, and I took him to his new home. His new mother thanked me for walking him, and I told her that I knew I no longer needed to walk him because he was in their home. I gave her the key to her father's home. I walked Barkley into the back of their home, and we all went into the screened porch area. I told them what dog food Barkley was eating as the container of dog food had no bag in it or label on the container. I also demonstrated the Sporn no-pull-halter collar that I had used to walk Barkley since I first started walking him four years earlier. I also answered her questions about arthritis in a dog. I suggested giving Kwai or Kyolic garlic tablets.

Then came the hardest part of all—saying goodbye to Barkley. I sat on the floor, held his face, and kissed his nose. I told him, "I never want you sick or sad, and I never want to be without you. If you need me or you think of me, I'll know."

Right after I left, I remembered I had left my leash on the table on the screen porch. I know that the husband and wife were within earshot. I walked back and asked if I had left my flexi leash in there. They replied yes. I opened the door and stepped inside with one foot to get the leash. Then Barkley got up and came to me. He wanted to leave with me. It tore me apart! I again knelt, took his face in my hands, and rubbed my face all over his beautiful face and told him he had to stay. I loved him very much and always would.

I pulled out of the driveway and headed home. Don's sudden death sunk into my reality. I wished he had not died. I had liked Don very much. He had always been happy, and he had adored Barkley. That was good enough for me.

There would be no Don going away on broadcasting trips that had lasted weeks and trips to Vegas to play the slot machines, so I wouldn't be seeing my dear Barkley. My life had changed in a huge way. I cried as I drove. I thought about how I had been hissing and fussing about pet sitting and wanting to write. I had been saying that for many years at that point. Gas prices were rising, but it was always difficult to raise pet sitting rates. Don had been thunderstruck when I told him that. He had asked if I would still come to see Barkley, and I had replied, "Of course I will!" But pet sitting is not a business that you set a date to end and then say goodbye - not if you adore the sweethearts as much as I do.

I got home and took my sweethearts for a walk. I thought about my last few hours with my dear Barkley. I needed closure on the old life even more than Barkley needed to take one final walk around the old neighborhood. I believe that Barkley knew I needed those three hours with him. Out with the old and in with the new; a new year would start in just a few days. In spite of all my bitching and moaning about having to get up early to walk someone else's dog and not having any days off, it still hurt to cut the cords.

I was grateful that I had taken a dozen beautiful photos of my dear, beautiful, gorgeous Barkley. I put one of them in the *Tropical Breeze Newspaper* with one of my "Ask Nanny Fran" columns. I gazed at them whenever I began to miss him. Animals are the beautiful ones while we people are the ugly ones. Little did I know.

But by January 5, 2008, so much had transpired. I had Barkley with me! About a week earlier, Don's daughter had called me. She was very distraught. Evidently, Barkley was not happy at her home. Go figure. First of all, everyone there was emotionally in shambles, and Barkley had been shaken to his core, so what did anyone expect from the parties involved?

Don's family was arranging to get Don's body to Canada for a viewing. I learned from a Canadian friend that Don, a Canadian himself, was very well known and beloved sportscaster. I was told that one station had an hour-long documentary on his life.

I am sure that the energy from those three individuals in the new home was totally disconcerting to dear Barkley. His father, his best friend, was nowhere to be found, and he was indeed confused particularly living with those two dachshunds.

A few days before the New Year's, I got a distress call from Don's daughter: "Francene, I need help with Barkley." He had startled them with some unusual behavior. I will admit that an eighty-four pound golden lion could do that easily if he desired, but Barkley did not desire that. He was just confused, and the people around him did nothing to soothe his sorrow over the loss of Don. Besides, he didn't know the strange woman who had just flown in from Canada. He also was growing weary of the constant yapping of the two dapple dachshunds. In his previous home, it had been quiet—just him and Don. And his new house was small. I imagined poor Barkley thought he had landed in hell.

I knew they were clueless about what to do with Barkley, so I asked, "Do you want me to take him off your hands?" I made the offer only because I knew that I had an empty condominium I could put him in if the weather got warm.

They said, "Oh yes! You're an angel!"

I drove to their home and went to the screened porch. There on the table were two pieces of paper I had requested. They said that Barkley was then in my care and that any medical treatments would be at my expense. (okay, okay…why did I write up an agreement that stated without question that any medical treatment would be MY expense!?!

I wrote that in specifically because I feared that one of the family members might conjure up a story that would make it believable that Barkley needed to be killed.) Yes, indeed I did. People will often conjure up a story to "get rid" of an animal that they do not like, find annoying, find inconvenient or costly. Yes, people indeed will. Ask any veterinarian about the stories they have heard.

Don's daughter had put something in the document that said that I would keep him if she didn't find other accommodations for him. The "other accommodations" for him scared the stuffing out of me. *What does other accommodations mean?* I was afraid she might give him to the humane society or some other animal league or put him down.

After that particular sentence, I wrote, "… that Francene approves of." I wanted to stay in the loop. Don's family was clueless about rescue groups, humane societies, and so on. Barkley had never been boarded, and he hadn't lived with other dogs before that. I could just see him stressed out living in a kennel with strange barking dogs and strangers. I was afraid he would bite someone there and be put down.

If that didn't happen and he were adopted out, I knew that the humane society of North Pinellas didn't have adequate staff to follow up with home checks other than phone calls … maybe! I was scared witless for Barkley.

I took him home. I asked a friend of mine who was a computer wiz to put together a flyer for me. I had originally driven to Kinkos with the photos copied to a disc and asked the personnel there if someone could spend five minutes with me to put together a simple one-page flyer with two pictures. Oh heavens no! I'd have to filled out a work order explaining everything I wanted done and then leave the order with the disc with the pictures. Then maybe, they would be ready in a day or two. Such a big deal! I walked out of there distraught. I was also pissed off.

Geesh, I could have moved a mountain all by myself in the time frame they gave me to conjure up the flyer I requested!!!

A colorful flyer was the only way Barkley would be attractive to anyone. His picture in black and white in the *Tropical Breeze Newspaper* would have no impact at all. I pondered this dilemma while driving home.

It suddenly dawned on me that a terrifically capable friend of mine could put this flyer together in a heartbeat. I called her and begged, pleaded, and promised my firstborn if she could do me this favor. I told her that I had about twenty beautiful pictures of Barkley and that I wanted at least two in the flyer, which I planned to disseminate all over the county.

It took her five minutes to create a beautiful flyer, which she emailed to me. I emailed it to Kinkos and had them print up three hundred color copies at 49¢ cents each. I wrangled a 10 percent discount on top of that because I was a Sam's Club business member.

Barkley and I drove to Kinko's for the beautiful flyers. We drove all over Pinellas County (Palm Harbor, Clearwater, Safety Harbor, and Dunedin) and even Hillsborough County (Tampa). We stopped at veterinarian offices, dog-grooming shops, pet food stores, and anywhere else seeking those who had a soft spot for dogs. I wheedled them into putting the flyer up on their bulletin boards.

I started walking Barkley at farmers' markets, fairs, and other places where he could meet people. I had lunch with him many times at outdoor cafes where dogs were allowed. All of this socialization was wonderful. Barkley loved everybody. While doing this and seeing how much Barkley loved meeting all kinds of people, I began to dislike the previous owner. I felt that not taking him out into public places was actually rather criminal.

My entire life was wrapped around Barkley. I put much of my personal and business life on hold, and I knew catching up would not be easy, but I was determined to get Barkley into a new home as quickly as possible.

I had my website designer put his face with a write-up on my website with a "click here for more information" button. I asked everyone I knew to go to my website to the Adopt-a-Pet page and email that page to everyone in their address books; exposure gets animals adopted. Look at the poor pups Michael Vick had; they were being socialized and loved and turned into pet therapy dogs. Media has power.

Sometime later, Barkley's aunt called to check on him. She apologized for not having gotten to me more quickly. I told her that my own sweetheart of eleven years had gone to heaven and that taking care of Barkley was filling a void in my life. I didn't have the luxury of collapsing and being worthless to all humanity for any length of time because of grief.

Grief can come when it's least expected, and it can hit hard and hurt like hell. My little girl and I had fought her cancer for over four years; I had spent over $50,000 with all the chemo and surgeries. I had to refinance my home and pull equity out to pay off credit card bills, but I don't regret spending that money or having $20,000 in credit card debt.

I told her about the flyers and said I'd drop one off with her. I did, but I heard nothing from her after that.

I'd spent nearly $500 for gas and printing the flyers. I spent hours and hours distributing the flyers. My pet-sitting business was relatively quiet then, so I had the time, but not much money was coming in. I was paying $1,500 a month for a vacant condo, Barkley's doghouse. I was spending on carpeting, plumbing, and window treatments to get the condo ready to be rented all with peanuts from my pet-sitting business. Barkley's Aunt, Uncle and Grandmother should have understood that even for angels, bills needed to be paid. I guess out of sight, out of mind. They were probably hoping that the next phone call from me would be that Barkley had a new home. This was another "dump the dog on the pet sitter" situation. Yes, dogs and cats are "dumped" on pet sitters all the time.

One of the bullshit aspects of this entire scenario was that Barkley had to sleep in my van because of my condo rules about dogs Barkley's size and because if he were there alone, noises from neighbors could set him off barking for hours and I wouldn't know about that until someone complained. At least he was right there in my van, so I didn't have to drive anywhere to walk him each morning and night.

One time when I went to PetSmart with him, everyone remarked about how beautiful he was. The next time I hear anyone say, "Oh, he is *sooo* beautiful. He'll find a home right away!" I'll shoot him or her.

One woman with two chows followed me out to my car to get a business card. I opened the door, and he hopped in. She saw his food and water bowl on the floor and asked if he was living there. I said yes. At night, it was quite cool. In the daytime, he was in my vacant condo with air conditioning. I could tell that she didn't approve.

Okay, folks, who the hell will step up to the plate here? Who the hell will spend 90 percent of each day driving around the town marketing Barkley, socializing Barkley, walking Barkley, and feeding Barkley while no one is contributing one penny toward his care or one minute of time to market, socialize, or love dear Barkley. However, everyone can and does judge!

Okay people, so I'm not doing this right? Do you want 24/7 responsibility for an eighty-four pound dog who has more hair than three dogs put together? Do you want to take him into your home? By the way, you cannot have a cat in your home and possibly not a dog. Whether he gets along with other dogs is still up for grabs. Maybe he will and maybe he won't. How about you becoming a twenty-four-hour foster home for him?

As I sit here typing, Barkley is lying on the tile floor sound asleep. What a dear—totally happy, relaxed, and safe. I hate to wake him up, but I need to get him into my car and drive to my own condo. It's nine at night. I have to eat dinner and walk him and then my two small dogs. Remember, I live in a condominium with no backyard. I'd love to be able to just stand there in my nightgown and slippers and tell them to go tinkle in the yard. No, I have to be dressed and actually walk all three of them.

My chiropractor called me and said a client had a pet-finder business and was trying with all her might to find Barkley a new home. God bless them … They were so kind!

After three months, I did find Barkley a wonderful couple who absolutely adored him. After he had been with them a few months, I visited and saw the most beautiful Barkley I had ever seen. He was supposedly a golden retriever and chow mix, and this couple had let his beautiful coat grow out magnificently and had brushed his coat until it was a golden blanket on him. He was absolutely gorgeous.

photo of Barkley with his new parents

Barkley B. Bearykins and his new mother and father

I tell my animals I will love them for forever and eighty-two more forevers. I obviously do or I wouldn't have committed over three months of my life to this beautiful child.

My dearest HRH Amelia Elizabeth chose to leave at this time. I felt she chose this time because I was so involved with rehoming Barkley. She knew that even though I would be totally devastated, I would carry on because Barkley needed me. I was all he had.

After Barkley found his new home, Amy's absence hit me like a thunderbolt; I walked around numb for months. I felt I was mute and walking through life getting things done that had to be done. I was a robot walking and bumping into walls. The most certain thing about grief is that it cannot be avoided, shortened in duration, or skipped over. Grief is an absolute must-do experience.

Chapter 40

Animal Communication

For five years, I wrote "Ask Nanny Fran," a monthly newspaper column. I always tried to impart information about animals that would help animals and their caregivers. Animal communication is one of the tools I recommend whenever you may have questions. In the column, I would ask and answer questions. Here's one of my columns.

Question: Do you work with animal communicators?
Answer: Yes, indeed! Over the years, I have taken classes in animal communication with animal communicators. I have several books in my home library written by animal communicators from all over the world. I have recommended them to my clients and other pet sitters as well.

In six months, I lost three dear friends. Animal communication has saved my life. The grief was profound ... and still is. Grief takes a circuitous course. It doesn't come one day and envelop you for a day, a week, or a month and then disappear. Oh no—it is much more insidious. When you least expect to be overwhelmed with the loss of your loved one, you will be blindsided.

A few days ago, I had to drive home, climb into my bed with a box of tissues, and let my heart, mind, soul, and body be racked by uncontrollable sobs. Yes, me. The strong one. The Nanny Fran Can person you all know. You all know my passion for all the animals and how strong I can be in any crisis situation. Yes, this was the same Nanny Fran who can or at least tries to seize victory from the jaws of defeat every time!

In my darkest hour, I reached out to my animal communicator friend. I thank God that she answered the phone. I needed help. I sobbed into the phone, "Judie, I'm losing it. I'm crumbling." I described how I had tried to be strong over the past few months. I described how I understood that the spirits of my dear ones were always around me and watching over me. However, the mind plays tricks, and once I started thinking about what I could have done and should have done, the grief washed over me like a tsunami.

I was comforted more than I can describe by her words. I shall always cherish her wonderful ability. I need to tell you at this point that you and I *can* do what she and other animal communicators do. Yes indeed, each one says that we all have the same ability. It is a matter of training.

I have recommended that other pet sitters telephone them. One of my pet sitter friends was distraught one evening and telephoned me. She could not imagine why in the world one of the several puppies in her client's home was frightened of her. Obviously, this would not do; pet sitters needed to attach leashes to dogs' collars to walk them.

She called my animal communicator friend, who was able to calm her fears and create harmony in the home. My pet-sitter friend was indeed grateful.

Along with books written by animal communicators, I have read *Animals and the Afterlife,* a wonderful book by Kim Sheridan, who is passionate about all creatures and has assembled incredible stories and information for all of us.

Yes, of course, over twenty years I have been there for many of you. We have wept together with our hearts in shreds. However, since I cannot be there for everyone 24/7 for forever, I recommend reading Kim's book.

I will not begin to list all of my babies who have passed on and then come back to me in the beautiful body of another dog or cat. However, most assuredly, they do come back. At this point in my life I look into the eyes of a dear one and ask them who they were before this life.

Over twenty years ago an animal communicator told me the following. "As you grow older Francene many of the animals you cared for will pass on and then come back to you. They will come back to you because in many instances you loved them more than their own families."

I was shocked (an elated of course) to hear this. My response was, "Oh my gosh, I am going to be a woman with a house full of animals!"

Twenty-six years later I can, without a doubt, confirm that what she said was totally true.

Chapter 41

Angels I Have Met

photo of the list of names of kittens

We meet angels everywhere, but many times, we don't recognize them.

One angel asked me to care for her puppy and two kitties when she and her husband traveled. I got to know this couple very well and adored them. Whenever I came to care for their three children, they always had several other kitties running helter-skelter through their home. For several years, they fostered wee kittens from the Humane Society of North Pinellas.

I never knew what I would find when I came—kittens already eating wet and dry food or tiny ones that needed bottle-feeding with KMR, kitty milk replacement powder, mixed with water and heated so that it would be similar to mother's milk. I was always so proud of all the babies this family loved and nurtured before allowing them to go back to the humane society to be adopted into forever homes.

I was always amazed at the names they gave each one. Each group of kittens got names of musicians, television personalities—you name it. Kellianne and Wayne were incredibly creative because they fostered over a hundred kittens yearly, and that would tax anyone's creativity.

I told Kellianne I was writing a book about pet sitting and wanted to include her in the book. I told her I had kept a list of the names of all the foster children she had taken care of in one year. She was elated and asked if I would forward her copies, and I did. I'm sure they brought back happy and sad memories. As we all know, we cannot save all of them. However, she and her husband spent countless hours for several years with a few hundred dear souls to ensure they were healthy and happy. God bless you, Kellianne and Wayne—I adore both of you!

I have so many precious memories of Jessica Elizabeth, Maggie, Marley, and the countless wee babies you loved and nurtured until they could find their own forever homes.

Many years ago Kellianne thought of a terrific title for my tall "tails".......Nanny Fran Off Leash"!

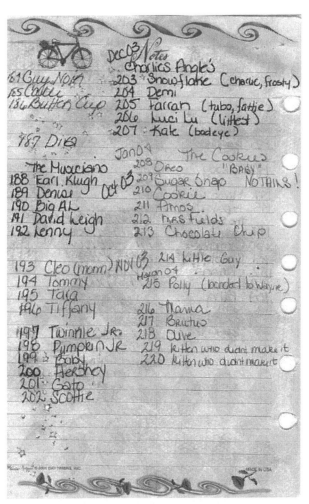

photo of the list of names of kittens

These lists of names are so adorable that I had to include one more list. You will see above that kittens 219 and 220 didn't make it. However, these babies were able to know incredible love, attention, and full tummies while they were in Kellianne and Wayne's loving arms. I direct your attention to the group named after cookies. How flippin' adorable!

Kellianne was the person who gave me the name Nanny Fran. Then, I was much younger and somewhat rejected it; after all, I wasn't old! But after a few years, I thought that I was naturally a Nanny Fran, and now, everyone knows me as Nanny Fran. I don't even have a last name.

Chapter 42

Teeth—Yes, Teeth

photo of Nanny Fran in cat face

Teeth have been the biggest expense I have had throughout life. I've had relationships with dentists that lasted longer than those I had with my two husbands. I've spent thousands of dollars over the years trying to keep my lovely teeth in my mouth. I supposedly have what is called soft teeth that are cavity prone. I cannot count the fillings, partials, root canals, and in more recent times implants I've had.

The bright side is that I never had to have wisdom teeth extracted because they were impacted. My dentist informed me many years ago that he believed my back molars were my wisdom teeth that came into my mouth quite easily because the molars had been pulled long ago. I was a dirt-poor Indiana farm kid who saw the dentist only when a tooth was absolutely killing me, and then it was pulled. Simple!

The wonderful part of having teeth like mine is that I never had to wear braces to straighten them because there was always room for one more.

One of my wonderful families had five Irish Wolfhounds and three Great Danes. The home was on two fenced acres, and it was lovely to run outside and play with all the babies. I used to stay overnight and sleep with their children when they would go on vacation.

Well, getting back to teeth ... Long ago, my dentist and I gave up on my back molars. They can hold just so many fillings before they are all metal and start to malfunction. Maybe thirty years ago, my dentist manufactured a completely metal partial that took the place of at least three molars. I'm still utilizing this fantastic piece of dental equipment.

My dentist had instructed me to take it out at night, so I'd put it on the bathroom sink. I did that during one of my sleepovers with the Great Danes and Irish Wolfhounds. The next morning, I let the dogs out for their morning tinkle and prepared their breakfasts. After that, I went into the garage. My sweetheart, HRH Amelia Elizabeth, had slept overnight inside my vehicle and she needed to have her morning walk. I always took her with me when I could. She was about a third the size of the Danes and the Wolfhounds, and it was their home, not hers; I didn't think it was wise to take her inside. We walked, I gave her breakfast, and helped her hop back into my jeep.

Inside, I saw one of the harlequin Great Danes lying on the floor intently studying something he had between his paws. I checked it out and nearly shrieked! He had my partial on the floor, and all I could see was him chewing on it and mangling it!

I snatched it off the floor and examined it thoroughly; it appeared to be exactly as I had left it the night before. I brushed it with my toothpaste and water to clean it and positioned it in my mouth. It was absolutely perfect. I was so relieved. It had cost me $1,500 way back then, twenty years earlier, and that was a lot. But actually, that came to $75 a year for an indispensable appliance. That dentist has retired; his appliance has outlasted him. I don't miss my ex-husbands, but I do miss him.

Dogs will often chew children's retainers because they smell like food. Makes sense to me, but the cost of replacing that device would have cost me three times what I earned at that house for a week.

Chapter 43

Unusual Pets and Unusual Pet Names

I once met a sweet Westie named Harley. The father explained that he had named him Harley because had decided that his Westie was the only Harley he was ever going to have.

I have also met a pig named Harley. I wondered why the name, and the owner explained that she had named her pig Harley because she was a hog. That explanation made sense to me.

I have known several Harleys who were harlequin Great Danes; that name seems to be as ubiquitous as naming a calico cat Callie. I have even done that once, but to my creative credit, I wish to inform you that her sister was named Smudge. The sister was identical to Callie except for a small black splotch on her sweet little nose, thus the name Smudge.

I have never cared for snakes. I always refuse to care for them because I tell the prospective client that I cannot bear to feed a living creature to another living creature. That's true, but I'm also petrified of them and want nothing to do with them. Over the years, my fears have lessened but not to the point that I can touch one.

Chapter 44

Thirty Feet of Reptiles

I remember one man inquiring about pet care. He thought that he might have to go into the hospital for surgery on his foot. He told me about his pets—six lizards each five feet long. They lived outside his home in his bird cage pool area and that I would be needed to visit once a day to remove all the newspapers that had been spread on the pool decking that had been soiled. I would need to place new papers down all over the pool decking and put down fresh water and food. The man had no idea I was envisioning thirty feet of *reptile* as he was explaining all that.

Not wanting to say, "Oh my God no! I can't do that for you!" I replied in a calm and businesslike tone, "I'm sorry, but I have no personnel to cover the area where you live." No way in the world could I walk into a birdcage pool area with six lizards each five feet long.

Hey, Jack Hanna, do you want this job? I'm only five feet and five inches tall myself!

Chapter 45

Thelma Lou

I always think of the movie *Thelma and Louise* whenever I think of Thelma Lou, a Chihuahua I met years ago. Her grandparents were caring for her while their son, Thelma's daddy, was out of town. During that time, the couple wanted to go away for two days. They called me to come for an interview so I could care for Thelma for those two days. I would be making visits to their home three times daily to feed, water, and walk her.

When I went into the home, I saw a small cat carrier on the floor; that was Thelma's crate. The lovely couple and I went into the living room; I sat on the couch with Thelma between me and the lovely woman. We talked about what was needed and on what days. They said Thelma was nervous around strangers, and she was. All the while I was there, Thelma was quivering and shivering as she stared at me. I told the couple that I didn't mind staying there talking for a good length of time to possibly take away some of Thelma Lou's fear of strangers. We talked and talked; the people were lovely.

A few days later, I was scheduled to visit Thelma Lou. When I walked in, I saw her in the cat carrier waiting for me. Thank heaven they had put her in there because she would have otherwise run and hid from me. I probably could never have gotten her on a leash in that event.

I opened the crate and snapped on her leash. I opened the back door to take her out into the backyard to tinkle. The back door opened onto a concrete slab. As I opened the door and started to take a step on to the concrete slab with Thelma, a black snake skittered across the far end of the concrete slab and disappeared into some bushes. I screamed just as I always do when I encounter a snake. You could hear my scream in Montana!

I settled down and looked at Thelma Lou. I wish I had a picture of her. That little dear was at the far end of her leash looking at me. The look on her face said, *Oh my God! What kind of a monster are you?* This poor dear was a nervous as Don Knotts on the *Andy Griffith Show,* and I had screamed at the top of my lungs; she had no idea why I had screamed, and she was petrified. We were trying to get to the point that poor little Thelma Lou could relieve herself, and I don't know why she hadn't when I screamed.

I decided I had no chance in hell of having her tinkle in the backyard with me. I went back in the home, shut the back door, and took Thelma to the front door. I thought that an entirely new area with no history of trauma might do the trick. She and I walked out into the front yard, and I stood quietly and patiently hoping she would relax and relieve herself. I lucked out. She tinkled, and we went back into the home. I fed her, put her back in the cat carrier, and said goodbye.

Later that evening, I got to Thelma Lou's home and found her in the cat carrier safe and sound. I knelt and opened the door on the carrier. Thelma Lou just stood there and growled at me. No movement forward. She stood her ground inside her safe place and growled ferociously. I was not about to put my hand inside. No point in grabbing her and traumatizing her even more than I had on the first visit.

I had no choice but to be honest and call the lovely couple and explain the situation. I don't know how they handled it from that point forward because that is when I left the assignment. Sometimes, you need to walk away. No point in further traumatizing an already nervous dog I had just sent leaping off a psychological cliff.

I realized I could have offered to place the carrier in a bathroom on some tinkle pads. At least then I could have come and gone as needed to give her fresh food.

Chapter 46

A Harley with a Purple Corvette Convertible

I grew up on a farm and had a pig named Oscar, so when a request came in for me to visit a home with a Vietnamese pot-bellied pig, I went.

I met a woman with the pot-bellied pig and a kitty. My first question was, "Where and how does this pig go to the bathroom?" The streets were lined with trees and one-story ranch style homes—no farmland in sight.

She said her front yard had a three-foot-tall concrete block wall that surrounded 95 percent of her front yard. She demonstrated how she took Harley outside to tinkle. She carried a broom. She admonished me not to walk in front of Harley because Harley might try to bite me if she was behind me. Interesting that I didn't walk away at that moment, isn't it? She never told me why she carried the broom but I definitely knew exactly why!

We three walked out front; I asked her what she might say to Harley to encourage Harley to do her business. She demonstrated by saying, "Harley, make boo boo." I didn't laugh; I'm very stoic and a fine actress. I observed, and we three walked back into her home. The thought in my mind at that time was, *Yeah, sure!*

Her home was undergoing a kitchen renovation, so things were stacked hither and thither and yon all over the home. I was shown an upholstered sofa that had a goose-down comforter on it; that was Harley's bed.

She introduced me to her kitty and showed me where the litter box was. Of course it was hidden in another room, and the direct path to it was blocked by large cardboard boxes. Evidently, Harley also liked to clean the litter box just as any dog in the home would.

I received feeding instructions for Harley and the kitty—so much of this and so much of that. Then I was shown several boxes of Wheaties and a large supply of raw carrots and apples—Harley's treats.

She wanted me there at some ungodly hour in the morning; I explained I was also doing overnight pet sitting at another home and visiting yet another in the early morning, so getting there at 5:30 a.m. was a bit much. We then agreed on a time that worked a good deal better for me.

She gave me a key and the dates she was going to be in Las Vegas. Thank heaven it was only about four days because as it turned out, I was happy when that assignment ended.

I found out on the first visit that the first order of the day would be to take Harley outside to tinkle. Well, broom in hand, I attempted to call sweetly to her so she would walk in front of me to and through the front door and into the front yard. God knows how I pulled that one off, but she did go outside. I noted that from time to time, she would make a U-turn and look menacingly at me. She especially seemed angry when I said, "Harley, make boo boo." Yikes, I was only doing what I had been told. Obviously, this pig was Queen of Everything and wanted me to be well informed of that.

We went inside; I fed her the prescribed amounts of food and then looked for the kitty. While I was feeding the kitty and scooping the litter box, Harley kept coming up to me for more food. There I was trying to spend time with the kitty and care for her properly as well, and here was this pig! Imagine me tossing handfuls of Wheaties on the floor to placate Harley so I could spend time with the kitty.

On one visit, I discovered I could step into the next room over cardboard boxes with the kitty in my arms and love and play with one her. Harley figured out how to bulldoze the boxes out of her way. No way was she coming to see me because I was her BFF—she wanted more food. I vacated the room with the kitty and went back into the kitchen. I threw down a few carrots and an apple or two to placate Harley. She was placated as long she was munching on a treat. I didn't spend a great deal of time on each visit because of that obnoxious and supposedly hungry pig.

All I seemed to be doing was playing ring around the rosy with the pig circling the kitchen island and throwing down cereal and carrots just to make her happy. When I realized that was going to be happening every visit, I decided to take Harley outside to "make boo boo" and come inside and feed her before trying to locate and care for the sweet kitty.

I got a bright idea. I grabbed a bag of carrots, the broom, and the kitty and went into the bathroom off the kitchen. I wanted to have uninterrupted quality time with the dear kitty without Harley being such a pest. I started doing that, and on my last visit, I was doing that when the woman came home. She had seen my car outside and knew I was in the home. However, when she walked inside, I was nowhere to be found. When I heard her calling for me, I called out, "I'm in the bathroom." I opened the door carrying the kitty, the broom, and a bag of carrots. Interesting visual, isn't it?

I explained that I had done everything Harley required but that she wouldn't leave me alone while I tried to spend time with her dear kitty, thus, I had devised this plan of going into the bathroom. I don't know if she believed me, but it was the truth.

She asked how the visits had gone with Harley. I said everything had gone well. Well, the visits *had* gone well. I didn't mention that Harley seemed to want to bite me each time we went into the front yard to make boo boo.

The woman looked at Harley and said, "She put on weight!" Her tone of voice indicated that that wasn't good. She had been gone only three or four days, not a week or two. I couldn't believe her statement (remember, I'm an Indiana farm kid), and it was all I could do to not blurt out, "Lady, she's a pig after all!"

So whenever I drive around that area and see a purple Corvette convertible, I think of Harley. Harley's mother told me that Harley sat in the passenger's seat when they went for rides.

When all was said and done, this woman said she would recommend me to other owners of pot-bellied pigs, but to this day, I haven't received one request to come visit another pig. I consider myself blessed.

Chapter 47

More Animal Names

I have had cats, and one was named Julio and another Gallo. There have been many other creative duos I have met over the years, and they were quite clever. However, people, please stop naming every animal who is black and white Oreo. Not the least bit creative.

And for heaven's sake, don't name your dog Dog or your cat Cat. That tells me you have no respect or love for your dear animal. It also shows laziness. Yes, you were much too lazy to give a proper name any thought at all. The same goes for the dog names Buddy and Shadow— not one bit of creativity; every dog in your life is your buddy and your shadow if you love him or her and treat them properly.

I have Elizabeth Taylor, Prince William, Princess Diana, William the Conqueror, and JC, but not for Jesus Christ; JC was named after my great-grandfather Joseph Campbell Woolverton, who was also an author. I also have dogs named Jack and Jill, Amos, Elizabeth Ann, Patrick, Riley (Smiley Riley) and Whoopie, a happy party girl!

One of my clients named their golden retriever Dave. Excellent name. The husband's name was Bill, and one day, I called the family and said, "Hello, Dave," when the husband answered the phone. He said there was no Dave there, and I apologized for supposedly dialing the wrong number. The instant I hung up, I realized what I had done. I called back and asked for Bill; I explained that I was the one who had called, and I felt silly!

Joey Bag of Doughnuts

Joey Bag of Doughnuts was one especially dear small poodle. His mother and father had a retail store that sold puppies. They told me how tiny Joey got his very long name.

One day, a salesman came to the store. Joey's mother stayed up front to greet customers while Joey's father went into the back office to meet with the salesman. When they finished their meeting, they walked into the retail area. Usually, Joey, Bogey, and Rudy were all running around the store, but they couldn't find Joey. They started searching and lo and behold they found him.

When the salesman had arrived, he had inadvertently placed a bag of doughnuts on the floor and walked to the back office. No one noticed the bag except Joey. When they found him, his face was covered with powdered sugar and chocolate, so he was named Joey Bag of Doughnuts. The name was so darling because Joey was a tiny white poodle. One can easily imagine all kinds of chocolate, chocolate icing, strawberry fillings, and such smeared all over his mouth and paws as he enjoyed himself.

Chapter 48

People I Respect

Okay, there are darn few! However, I will never forget John Wayne. I didn't meet John Wayne, but I met his double.

Several years ago, some people in Tarpon Springs were trying to raise funds to create a dog park in the city. I was attending meetings and trying to help them. One fundraiser was a spaghetti dinner. At the time, I was advertising my pet-sitting business in a magazine that advertised all kinds of people and businesses involved with pets. I had a dynamite ad on the inside front cover. Whenever I attended any function, I passed out my business cards and copies of the magazine.

I walked into a lovely, old Victorian home in the historic part of Tarpon Springs for the dinner and saw a husband and wife I knew from prior meetings. I said hello and started passing out copies of the magazine with my ad. The couple introduced me to their son, who was a vet. I told him I was a professional pet sitter. This man was as tall and handsome as John Wayne and had a reserved and gruff way of speaking just like John Wayne. He was easily over six feet tall and was wearing all black, a rather imposing individual to a five-five woman like myself. However, I handed him a copy of the magazine, showed him my ad on the inside, and introduced myself. He just sat in his chair like a stone, and I don't think he even looked up at me when he stated, "I met a pet sitter once. She was pretty uppity."

I replied, "I don't know why because animals will reduce you to rubble in a heartbeat." I can't explain how or why that flew out of my mouth, but he loved it! He suddenly became personable.

He was a vet at Tampa Bay Downs, a racetrack, and we talked about the feral cats that lived at the race track; he said he had spayed and neutered them on his own. When he said, "It's only a little bit of string," I knew he was referring to sutures. I was in awe of this vet caring so much for the wee creatures that no others gave a damn about. What a good and great individual with a huge heart.

After dinner, I walked into the parking lot, and there he was in his pickup. He slowed down and stopped, and we chatted some more. He was proud of his truck, and we talked about how he had had to carry his office in his truck to the horses in their stables. He said something that really impressed me: "When I was going to school at Cornell [talk about a prestigious vet school], I asked my professor where I could do the most good as a vet, and he said at a race track."

Of course, so much money is at stake that unscrupulous, money-grubbing owners race horses when they shouldn't and many times end up killing them. No one has ever impressed me with his or her genuine caring for the animals that came before money and fame. I hope this wonderful human being is still out there doing good for the animals he comes in contact with.

All over the world, people are caring for animals that are abused and thrown away for a million reasons. So many people use their own money and time to feed, house, and provide food and veterinary care for homeless animals. Every day and everywhere in the world, people are searching out feral cats and dogs and feeding them daily. They seek no public funds for this though they might be eating ramen noodles to provide dog and cat food to homeless street babies.

As have so many others, I have spent many thousands of dollars to save the lives of many animals. I cannot add up all the vet bills I have paid on behalf of all the sweethearts who have passed through my arms. I am so blessed to have known every one, and I'm incredibly blessed with excellent health. Doctors don't know my name because I'm never ill. I'm so grateful to God for my health; that allows me to love and care for animals. I'm not wealthy, and I'm not a nonprofit organization that receives dollars from others.

I wouldn't have it any other way. So many things are not important to me including jewelry, makeup, fine clothes, expensive cars, and impressing other people. I am here for the animals. I know I'm walking the path I'm supposed to.

I know two women who each founded low-cost spay and neuter clinics for the animals. Each one adores the animals and wants to stop the slaughter. I am always referring people to their fine organizations so their sweethearts can get the care they need at an affordable cost. I'm proud of people who see the need and fire themselves up to meet it. These two women are kind, brave, and committed souls who care about the health, safety, and security of the animals. They've accomplished so much with their organizations over the years and have saved so many lives. God bless them and all their staffs.

Chapter 49

Amy's Angel Rest

Amy's Angel Rest came into existence in 1998. It was created accidently because I had no idea how many animals would need to find new homes from then on. The economy was not in a nasty predicament then, but humans were nonetheless throwing away animals.

In 1998, I moved into a two-bedroom condo with my dog and two kitties. As a professional pet-care provider, I came in contact with people who had animals, and from time to time, they needed to find them other homes. I had no idea how much of this would become a regular event in my pet-care career.

My condo complex limited residents to two animals that couldn't weigh more than fifteen pounds. As time progressed, I blew through that rule and carried on. Thank heaven, God protected me throughout my twelve years there.

The first time I broke that rule was when my computer repairman decided to go to the Iraq War. He and his girlfriend, who was planning on moving back into her mother's home, had over time taken in nine cats. Paul's computer repair business put him in contact with many people. Some of those people had cats they wanted to get rid of; that's how Paul and his girlfriend ended up with nine. His girlfriend's mother wouldn't accept that many cats. That was something the average person would say. Paul was thinking about taking all nine to the animal shelter, and that filled me with dread.

At that time, many people were dumping their animals at animal shelters and going off to war. I knew that the shelters were overflowing and that many of the animals would not be adopted, particularly the older ones. Most of them would have to be put down to make space for incoming animals. That broke my heart; I couldn't bear the thought.

I put the nine kitties in my second bedroom. Paul and his girlfriend knew that I'd take good care of them. I told them all that I loved and valued them. Over time, they of course came out of the bedroom and occupied the condo with me and my dog and cat. My screened porch was ideal for them. I spent some money on pet-defense screening, and it was worth it. Cats tend to climb on screens after lizards or birds on the outside. With that screening, my heaviest kitty could climb onto the screen and not create even the smallest hole or rip.

I was coming and going several times daily to care for animals; I'd stop at my place to care for my animals and leave again. I loved that my kitties could enjoy the outside but in the safety of my screened porch. Anyone walking by could see my cats on the porch, but since they were all inside and not bothering anyone, I thought all would be well. However, rules are rules, and every condo complex has at least one person who's always complaining about something. I was unlucky enough to meet up with one of those unhappy souls while walking my two dogs.

She was walking her Yorkie; we met each other at the mailboxes. We exchanged pleasantries, and at one point, she looked down at my two dogs and glanced in the direction of my condo. Of course the kitties sitting out in my screened porch were readily apparent.

I knew what was coming. She said, "You have two dogs and several cats, and—" I stopped her in midsentence because I knew that she would tell me about the two-animal limit. I said, "Oh yes. I take in feral cats from the humane society. I keep them for several months to socialize them, and then I give them back to be adopted." That was a total lie I conjured up in a nanosecond. I was proud. I looked like an angel, Mother Teresa. Brilliant!

I never heard a word from anyone after that. I totally amazed myself because for the first twenty years of my life, I stuttered, and speaking extemporaneously as I had done with her was impossible for a person who stutters. I had surprised myself. I had not stuttered in the past forty-three years, but under stress, I could have broken down and done so.

Anything for the animals—that's my attitude. I have been accused of being that kind of person on several occasions.

Pet-care people automatically become rescuers as well as groomers and trainers. People approach you with anything and everything to do with animals once they find out you love animals and are involved with them daily.

George, Samantha, Amelia, and Elizabeth

One afternoon, I received a phone call from a young mother. She told me, "Francene, can you help me? Someone in my neighborhood found a box with four kittens at her door. They're only a few weeks old. They've been handed from house to house because no one has the knowledge or time to feed and care for them."

She told me people were trying to feed these tiny kittens dry cat food! At their age, only KMR, kitty milk replacement, three times daily was the right food for them. Somehow, this young mother ended up with these four babies and was hand-feeding them three times a day. That doesn't sound like such a huge commitment of time and energy until you actually do it. I've done it, and it requires a huge commitment of time, patience, and love. She told she was breastfeeding her youngest, had a toddler, two dogs, and a husband who was recovering from a back injury. She was overwhelmed. She asked me if I could take them, and how could I say no?

I picked them up from her and took them to a clinic to have them checked for several possible diseases, and they all were extremely healthy. Thank heaven for that—they had already had a tough start in life.

My condo had two bedrooms. I had set up a litter box on the floor of the main bath and put towels folded on the floor for kitty beds so the little ones could rest. I bought some KMR as well as baby bottles to feed them. I warmed some water, mixed some KMR in it, and put it in the baby bottles. I sat on the floor, and all four kittens came running at me fighting to eat! Poor dears, they were starving. I maneuvered as quickly as I could from one to another until all four had full tummies. The walls and floor of the bathroom and I were covered in sticky KMR. I had some cleaning to do, but I also had four very happy kittens.

Sounds overwhelming and tiring, right? Well, I did that three times a day for the next two months. I also had to keep the litter box fresh. I'd move it to one bathroom so I could clean the other, and then I reversed that process. I couldn't leave them in my master bedroom bath as getting up in the middle of the night to tinkle would have awakened all four of them and they would have expected to be fed—not possible when I was half-asleep.

Eventually, I started letting them eat wet kitty food and playing on the screened porch. They were so tiny. One fell asleep next to the case for my sunglasses and I noted that the case and the wee one were the same size.

They were darling. I named the boy George, a good, solid, male name. Two of the kittens were tuxedos; I named one Elizabeth Taylor because she was so beautiful, and I named the other Amelia Elizabeth after my border collie I had adored for twelve years. Amelia Elizabeth was black and white as all tuxedo kitties are, but she also had a thin white stripe down the middle of her nose that reminded me of the same white stripe my sweet HRH Amelia Elizabeth Border Collie had down the middle of her forehead that ran down to her nose. The last female was solid black. I named her Samantha I guess after the TV series with the witch named Samantha.

When they were old enough, I took them to be spayed or neutered. At age two, George had to have emergency surgery. His penis was malformed from birth, and we had all hoped that Mother Nature would straighten things out for him. But he was about to die if he didn't get an emergency operation. His kidneys, bladder, and urethra were all blocked and swollen. I rushed him over to Florida Veterinary Services in Tampa. They performed emergency surgery on him and gave him twenty-four-hour supervision for five days. I visited him several times day and night.

Poor dear! Thrown away, rescued, and then sitting at the edge of heaven all alone in a strange place in pain with all kinds of strangers poking and prodding him with strange and nasty medications and needles. I made sure he knew he was loved and had a family.

The cost of the surgery and several days of twenty-four-hour care came to $6,000. That was the second time I had adopted a stray that ended up needing emergency surgery. Jack and George had had surgeries at that facility to the tune of $12,000. Damn it all—why wasn't I a nonprofit, or a Rockefeller, or a Melinda Gates?

The first animal was a black dog named Jack. Jack and George are still with me. The people at FVS knew me before meeting Jack and George. Nearly ten years earlier, I had visited Florida Veterinary Services several times over four years to eradicate cancer from my Border Collie rescue sweetheart, HRH Amelia Elizabeth. She had twelve surgeries, twenty chemo treatments, and twenty-five radiation treatments. If I hadn't had credit cards, I couldn't have persisted in treating her cancers. I ended up with the worst credit score possible.

Beau and Sophie

Another family had a death. The husband and wife had a dog, and just before the husband's death, they had adopted two kittens from the Suncoast Animal League. This death was totally unexpected, and the wife was in shock.

She decided to sell their condo and move to the East Coast to live with her father, but his condo complex didn't allow animals. She got letters from her doctor and psychiatrist stating that her dog was a therapy dog, which allowed her to have her dog in the condo. However, the two kittens wouldn't be allowed. She asked me to take them in, and of course I did. I've had the kitties for three or more years but have lost touch with the woman.

I decided that no one should live in a complex that doesn't allow animals. We never know when a friend or family member may have a need to live with us and may have a need for an animal. It seems that many more people are recognizing animals as healers and therapy for all kinds of ailments people might have.

I truly am convinced that raising a child without a pet amounts to child abuse. When the entire world has told a child that he or she has done something wrong and is banished to a room without TV or computer, he or she needs unconditional love from a puppy, kitty, bunny, or other good buddy.

In 2010, my life underwent some major changes and I moved into a single-family home with a large yard with three dogs and fourteen cats. I'd blown a large hole in the two-animals rule at the condo. Thank heaven the maintenance man there was an animal lover; he acted as a cushion between me and the board members. He reassured them that he had been in and out of my condo on many occasions and that I had a very clean and nice home. I'm so grateful that he was there for me because other busybodies with no lives were always putting their noses into everyone else's business. Sad. After having lived in a condo, I knew that I would never want to do that again.

So Amy's Angel Rest continued in a new location. Over the years, I have lost a few kitties. One developed liver cancer; the vet told me there was nothing I could do. He went to heaven. One morning, I found another one dead on my floor. I imagined that was due to a heart attack or aneurysm. When animals are rescued, you have no idea of their age, parentage, and other such information. Even if you take the best care you can of kittens or puppies, they can still suddenly pass on to heaven and you'll have no idea what went wrong.

Funkie and Sunshine

I have given a home to two beautiful cats that had been dumped out at a restaurant. The owner of the restaurant was feeding a colony of ferals every day, and she noticed two that had obviously been dumped. She could tell they weren't feral because they were very loving. I went to get them, and I still have them. One of them had been front declawed. Imagine how heartless a person has to be to declaw a cat and then dump it. The second cat is an awesomely beautiful Maine coon cat. I named him Funkie after a kitty I had cared for and adored who was also a Maine coon named Funkie.

Nikki

I took in a nineteen-year-old keeshond. Yes, nineteen. I have paperwork from the vet that established her age. One friend had a daughter in a high school vet program, and she and her classmates took turns with a dog that an elderly person couldn't care for any longer, but none of the students' families could take the dog in permanently, so my friend asked me to take her in.

So now I have a nineteen-year-old, loving, perfectly healthy sweetheart who happens to be deaf, but deaf is no big deal. She gets along famously with the other animals in my home, and she absolutely adores me. She's under me all the time whether I'm sitting or standing just staring adoringly at me. I'm so glad she's safe and happy. She's perfectly healthy and lovely.

After I moved into my new home, I got a call from a rescue organization to take in a dog. I've since taken in three dogs from them—all elders that needed a safe home. The first sweetheart was a chow named Bear, a real love who was later diagnosed with a huge cancerous tumor in his abdomen. We had to let him go to heaven. The second was a beagle that eventually showed pitiful Alzheimer's signs and walked aimlessly all over and had no idea what planet she was inhabiting. We eventually had to let her go to heaven.

The third needed a new home because her family was being evicted. She was a golden retriever and basset hound mix—she looked like a short-legged golden retriever. That was Whoopie, whom I had mentioned earlier—a real delight.

I'd been told she had been spayed, but that wasn't the case, so I had to have her spayed. One time, I noticed an odd growth on her. Thank heaven I was observant. She had a raging infection that would have killed her if she hadn't been operated on. She sailed through the procedure and became a total puppy at age sixteen or seventeen. I spent about $1,500 on her spaying and operation. I'm not rich; I had to pull money out of savings. However, I'm rich and incredibly blessed in other ways—I have absolutely excellent health. I'm totally flexible and mobile without even aspirin. I feel God keeps watch over me so I can be available for the animals.

I don't eat properly and never take vitamins, but I never get sick as opposed to many others I know who have allergies and are on several medications. I go to doctors for emergencies only. I stay away from corn and wheat in all my cat food and dog food. I would rather buy good food and keep them healthy and away from vets. I've spent thousands of dollars fighting cancer with a precious dear, and I don't ever want to walk that path again.

Mercedes or Lady Cedes

One time, I heard of a lovely female puppy that had been found in a cornfield in Clewiston, Florida and then taken to the Miami Dade Animal Services, a well-known slaughterhouse. A rescue group had pulled her, and she needed a foster home. One Sunday afternoon, I drove to Miami, loaded this sweet dear into my car, and drove back to Clearwater. The poor dear was so frightened that she crouched down, looked at me, and wouldn't move. With gentle handling and the unbelievable, loveable energy from Patrick, my Australian Shepherd, who is the same age as Mercedes, she has blossomed.

It's such a joy to watch them run and play in the backyard; you would think they were littermates. Patrick weighs forty-two pounds and Mercedes weighs 50 pounds. Both are energetic and loving. Getting these two soul mates together was the best thing I've ever done.

Patrick

Patrick was a rescue from Pasco Animal Control. Because they were at one time fifty dogs over their limit there, instead of commencing a slaughter, they offered free adoptions. I went there to foster an older German shepherd with medical issues so I could free up a space for another dog. When I arrived, I learned he had been killed, so I decided to bring home another baby. I walked through the kennels and saw this lovely black dog with brown stockings on all four legs. He was beautiful. I think he reminded me of a black dog I had grown up with on the farm back in Indiana. Her name was Old Pat, who was my dearest friend then.

They told me he was a stray; there was a four-day hold on strays in case someone came to claim him. He had three more days to go before they could adopt him out. I placed my name on him and went home and prayed no one would claim him. Well, no one did, but they said they needed to neuter him before they could release him. I tried to talk them into letting me get him neutered, but I couldn't, so he stayed there another week and a half.

Just as I knew he would, he contracted an upper respiratory infection there. When I brought him home, I had to keep him separated from my other dogs and give him medication twice daily. I did; he got over the upper respiratory, and he's been in wonderful health ever since.

Chapter 50

Nanny Fran Can ... With Nanny Alice's Help

This is an incredible story about Molly. Molly died. Well, not really. But, yes indeed, Molly died. There was even a small wooden urn with her ashes inside and a brass plate on top reconfirming that Molly was indeed loved and missed.

Molly was a darling black Cocker Spaniel who was very mild mannered, sweet, and loving. I first met her when her mother asked me to come and interview with her about Molly's care. I drove the thirty minutes from my home to Molly's home and met with her mother, who was single and in extraordinarily ill health for a young woman. She weighed about two hundred pounds, had diabetes and a heart condition, had had one leg amputated below the knee, and was a smoker.

She said her doctor had recommended she undergo a procedure— holes would be made through her heart, which would in turn increase blood circulation through the heart. I had never heard of that operation. I could tell she was frightened at the prospect of such surgery. She asked, "If I die, will you euthanize Molly and bury her with me?"

Talk about being taken aback. I was stunned. However, I replied yes. Between you, me, and the fence post, of course I wouldn't have done that. However, I wanted to step up to the plate immediately because there was a possibility that if I said no, I wouldn't become Molly's caregiver. I didn't want another pet sitter to do that to dear Molly.

I began caring for Molly whenever the young woman had to go into the hospital. She lived in a senior condo community; she had inherited her place from her parents. She lived about forty-five minutes from me, so visiting Molly three times daily involved an hour and a half of driving each time, and I always tried to spend at least an hour with each sweetheart, so this commitment alone took about six hours out of my day. No matter what the fee was, there was no profit left after these trips.

I was called upon more and more to walk Molly I eventually suggested that whenever Nancy went to a nursing home for care or the hospital, Molly could stay with me and my fur children and have more people time, love time, and play time with my dogs. Nancy agreed to that.

Molly was a delight; she rode with me and my sweetheart Amelia Elizabeth all over town. We had a grand time together. I would take her home whenever Nancy got back.

Over time, Nancy's hospitalizations became more frequent. She was smoking and eating greasy food, not in the best interests of a diabetic. Her calls to me started consisting of, "I'm home now. Bring Molly home," like a barked command, and that annoyed me. I was also annoyed to discover that Molly had a urinary tract infection or another condition at another time that had not been treated.

I took Molly to my vet for all her county shots, treatment for her urinary tract infection, and any other condition noted at the time. When an animal is given its county vaccinations, according to the county, the person who takes the animal to get those shots becomes the legal owner, but I kept that bit of information tucked away. When I did this, I knew that my vet knew what I had in mind; he said, "Francene has a big heart." He was right, but he kept his thoughts to himself, and I didn't intend to involve this dear man in any of my future schemes.

I couldn't let Molly suffer because her mother could not or would not treat her properly medically.

Nancy's visits to the hospital or nursing home for care became longer and longer, and Molly and I spent a great time deal of time together.

At this same time, Nanny Alice was also seeing animals with me. Alice was an incredible individual. She was a striking woman, slender, tall, and she had a short, man-style haircut. Her hair was salt and pepper, and her eyes sparkled or bore holes through you depending on her mood.

She was always quoting Greta Van Sustern and other news people from MSNBC, CNN, etc. to me. She also read at least two newspapers daily. Her spine was hard as iron and straight as an arrow. She was a no-nonsense, brilliant Yankee. However, she adored all animals. I believe she looked at most people as suffering fools. We had a great deal in common, and I adored her.

We often would go have lunch and talk. I loved her and valued our friendship. Whenever a call would come in for someone to visit kitties, I'd ask Alice if she wanted to meet the people and take the assignment. I tended to take all the dog-walking assignments as I was much younger. I told Alice about Molly's situation, and she became as incensed at it as I was.

I feared that one day, Nancy would be found dead in her condo and dear, sweet Molly would be whisked off to the pound. Not being a young, adorable puppy, I was afraid she wouldn't be adopted and would be euthanized.

One evening, I was at another client's home and their golden retriever and I were walking outside. All at once, this sixty-pound dog went down and couldn't stand. We were on the street in front of her home in a lovely gated community, but not a soul was in sight. I couldn't lift this sweetheart, and I was panicking. I called a vet tech friend to see if she could come and help me. I greatly appreciated her helping me get this beautiful golden girl up off the street and safe inside her home. She was a young girl, newly married, and I knew she and her husband were not awash with money, so the $50 I gave her was put to good use. Unfortunately, veterinary technicians are paid very little.

I was fuming because this lovely Golden Retriever was not being given the full dosage of Rimadyl, an anti-inflammatory for her arthritis, by her caregivers. Money was not the issue—they had lots—so how could they let their baby suffer? My heart was broken because she was in so much pain.

Then the call came. Nancy barked, "I'm home. Bring Molly back." It was nearly ten o'clock at night. I was at least thirty minutes from my home, where Molly was, so delivering Molly to Nancy would make my workday much too long. I told Nancy I'd bring Molly back in the morning, and I did.

These visits became more and more frequent, and Nancy began stalling with the money. I didn't care about the money anywhere near as much as I cared about Molly, my dear one. The stalling with the money meant to me that Nancy didn't have enough to properly care for Molly, who was not a chronically ill puppy but seemed to have frequent urinary tract infections and had a slight heart issue. I figured that Nancy wasn't taking Molly outside to tinkle or poo. Poor dear Molly was holding her urine and creating one infection after another.

I wondered about what I could do. My intuition told me that Nancy was going to leave this earth sometime in the near future. Trust me, I have learned to pay attention to my intuition. Infallible to the max!!!!

How do you whisk away someone's dog when that person is still alive? I came up with a plan—get Molly the next time Nancy requested and then tell her Molly had passed away in my care as she was napping. Hey, things like that happen all the time to animals and humans.

Alice and I went to a pet crematory and told them that my animal had died and that I wanted to have a lovely urn to put her remains in. Then, we went to a place in a mall that engraved all kinds of jewelry and mementos. I got a brass plate with the words, "Molly, I will always love you," which I affixed to the urn.

Okay, step three—ashes. I was a single woman in a condo who never used a grill. I got the bright idea to visit a family who had several fireplaces. I had been their pet sitter for years. Nanny Alice and I went to visit this couple.

When we arrived, I was shocked. The house had been gutted. All furniture and flooring had been removed. Workers were drilling holes into the ground beneath the home, inside the various rooms of the home, and filling them with concrete to stabilize the foundation. We talked with the husband and wife. I noticed that every fireplace in their home had been swept clean, damn it!

I thought of another possibility—the free-standing barbeque grills at Phillippe Park. We drove there and walked around the park. And walked. And walked. All the grills were in use; we had gotten there at dinnertime. All grills not in use were clean as a whistle!!!

I persisted. I visited a lovely young mother who would visit animals for me. She came out to my car, and I held up a plastic bag. Of course

I had a sparkle in my eyes when I asked, "If you have a barbeque grill, I'd appreciate some ashes in this bag."

She smiled; she knew I was up to something. She walked up the driveway and returned quickly with my bag filled with cold, grey ashes from her barbeque grill. I smiled a wicked smile, said thank you, and left. She was grinning from ear to ear and waving as I pulled away.

I went home and took the Pinellas County rabies tag, which was metal, off Molly's collar. I put the tag into the bag of ashes. I put the bag in the urn. I showed Alice the urn and a sympathy card in which I had described the unfortunate discovery of Molly when I had indeed thought she had been sleeping. I said all sorts of sweet, kind things and then put the card in an envelope and put the envelope into a bag with the urn.

I told Alice that I was so angry with Nancy that I couldn't convincingly walk up to her, hand her the bag, and offer my sympathy for her loss of Molly. I was still livid at her barked commands to me and her not taking care of Molly. Nancy had trod on my last nerve!

Dear Nanny Alice delivered the package and her condolences to Nancy the next day. She told me that she didn't think Nancy believed her, but I didn't give a rat's posterior about that; the deed had been done.

One day, I was at home when I heard a loud knock on my door. I glanced through my blinds and saw a short, stocky, brown-haired man in uniform who looked quite official. Ooops! Of course, Molly and Amy were barking. I knew I couldn't open the door without the two of them rushing the door. I felt that the gestapo man had come for Molly, so I took Molly and Amy to my bedroom.

I answered the front door, and the first words out of the officer's mouth were, "I'm not here about Molly." Of course he wasn't. Molly had all her vaccinations current, and I was registered as her current owner. Whew!

He said I was running a doggie day care from my condo and didn't have a license for that. Oh crap! I hadn't expected that. I realized Nancy was striking out at me any way she could think of. I explained to him that I wasn't caring for dogs in my condo. I told him I had my dog there as well as a client's dog that I was taking to the vet later that day. I'm a fast thinker/liar. Again, for the millionth time: "Anything for the animals."

He asked, "Can I see proof that this dog is owned by another family?" and I said, "Certainly." I ran to my desk, got paperwork for a black Labrador, and showed it to him. That seemed to satisfy him. Thank God I didn't have to show him the black Labrador, as a black cocker spaniel and a black Labrador look nothing alike.

After that, I kept getting notices that I had a registered letter to pick up at the post office, but I ignored them. Whenever I saw a small red car drive by, I was paranoid that it was Nancy looking for Molly.

I called Alice. She had always loved Molly and had offered to give her a loving, wonderful forever home. I took Molly to her, and everyone was blissful except for Nancy.

A few months passed, and Alice remarked that she wondered what Nancy was up to. She decided to pay a visit to Nancy's next-door neighbor and inquire about her; she learned that Nancy had been found dead on her kitchen floor with a Miniature Pinscher in her condo. The Min Pin had been whisked away to the humane society. She learned that Nancy's brother was the sole heir to the condo. He had the condo cleaned out and put up for sale. He cared nothing about Nancy's animals or belongings.

Alice said, "You knew Nancy was about to kick the bucket, didn't you?"

Yes, I had. I always trust my intuition.

Alice said that we had done the right thing for Molly as she would have gone to the humane society and because of her elder status might have been sent to heaven solely because of her age.

Once we knew that Nancy had crossed over, I could breathe easily. I no longer lived in fear of small red cars or short and stocky Mr. Nasty Pants gestapo agents pounding on the door of my condo demanding to see a dog.

Molly lived with Alice for several years, and they adored one another.

At this writing, Alice, Molly, and Nancy are all up in heaven probably getting along famously.

At least I understand that no one holds grudges up in heaven … I would like to believe it is true.

Many years ago I told God that I wanted to see, feel, and taste life. I didn't want to sit on the sidelines and watch it play out before my eyes. I wanted to participate. Well, he certainly granted my wish!

Made in the USA
Columbia, SC
05 March 2021